Words from the Wild

D1292400

Words from the Wild

Favorite Columns from *A Yankee Notebook*

WILLEM LANGE

Compiled and Edited by
GRACE LESSNER

BAUHAN PUBLISHING
Peterborough · New Hampshire
2015

Published for New Hampshire Public Television by Bauhan Publishing.

Library of Congress Cataloging-in-Publication Data

   Words from the wild : favorite columns from a Yankee notebook /
   Willem Lange ; compiled and edited by Grace Lessner.
      pages cm
   Includes bibliographical references and index.
   ISBN 978-0-87233-215-7 (alk. paper)
   1. Natural history—New England. 2. Hiking—New England—Anecdotes.
   3. Outdoor recreation—New England—Anecdotes. I. Title.
   QH105.N4L36 2015
   508.74--dc23

                        2015016225

PO BOX 117 PETERBOROUGH NEW HAMPSHIRE 03458

WWW.BAUHANPUBLISHING.COM
603-567-4430

Book design
Kirsty Anderson

Cover design
Henry James

Printing
Kase Printing

Cover Paper
Monadnock 120lb Astrolite Smooth

Text Paper
Monadnock 80lb Astrolite Smooth

MIX
From responsible
sources
FSC® C006892

NEW HAMPSHIRE
PUBLIC TELEVISION

nhptv.org

268 Mast Road
Durham
New Hampshire
03824

WINDOWS to the WILD

For outdoor adventurers—aspirational and actual—
and viewers like you.

Contents

Preface

I am very proud of *Windows to the Wild*, one of several locally focused programs from New Hampshire Public Television. In each episode, our intrepid, award-winning producers work with Willem Lange to tell special stories unique to our region, which is unmatched in its natural diversity and beauty.

Because NHPTV is the Granite State's public television station and community-supported, our focus is on serving our viewers and our state. This television series, now in its tenth season, speaks to our mission of engaging minds, connecting communities, and celebrating New Hampshire and New England.

We offer our deepest thanks to the Gilbert Verney Foundation and Monadnock Paper Mills, Inc., for their generous support, which made the publication of this book, *Words from the Wild*, possible.

We hope that this book will inspire you, as our television series has inspired so many viewers, to enjoy and appreciate the outdoors wherever you are.

—Peter Frid
President and CEO, New Hampshire Public Television

Moving along New England's natural corridors as we produce *Windows to the Wild* brings us face to face with people who stop Willem Lange and share their stories of why they are "out there." There's no better reward in our work than to hear a hiker talk about recovering from heart surgery because of the inspiration he found from our program, or to hear how a person uses the outdoors to deal with adversity, or to meet a family that recognizes Will and stops to share their own adventures in nature with him.

The goal of *Windows to the Wild* is to make nature accessible to everyone. We hope our program—and Will's book—will encourage our viewers and readers to embrace the outdoors and all its powers.

—Phil Vaughn
Executive Producer, *Windows to the Wild*

Whenever we're recording an episode of *Windows to the Wild,* we try to keep the hiking party moving at an average speed of one mile per hour. As Will's videographer, I'm constantly running ahead with the camera to catch him as he approaches scenic areas, and filming his conversations along the trail. No matter where we are, I'm always impressed with Will's ability to make people forget that a camera is documenting their every move. He's very adept at connecting with people of all ages and backgrounds.

At the beginning of each program, we do a setup shot with Will where he tells our audience what we hope to accomplish on that show. This book of Will's columns about our adventures in producing *Windows to the Wild* is like reading the behind-the-scenes, post-show story. Check the list at the back of the book for the episode that relates to each column. And be sure to tune in!

—Steve Giordani
Videographer and Producer, *Windows to the Wild*

Introduction

On one of my very first trips, probably in 1940, I saw an ostrich egg and a hummingbird egg side by side in a glass case. My great-grandmother used to lead my sister and me on trips every Wednesday to the natural history museum in Albany, New York, where we marveled at the skeleton of a mastodon, a rosy quartz grotto, and dioramas of past geological ages and Iroquois Indian life. On Thursdays, we went to Washington Park, with its statue of Moses striking the rock to get water and, in the shallows along the path by the lake, little sunfish eager for handouts.

That did it. I've been more or less thinking constantly ever since then about my next trip. My pals—a succession that goes back over seventy years—and I have roamed from the brooks and pastures of Central New York to the Adirondack and White Mountains and the Alaskan bush. In the past few years we've even canoed the Canadian tundra north of the Arctic Circle, but the old question remains the same: *What's next?* Be it next year or around the next bend.

In 2001, someone tipped me off that New Hampshire Public Television was holding auditions for a host an outdoor program called *Wildlife Journal*, which was coproduced by NHPTV and the New Hampshire Fish and Game Department. When that series ended in 2005, NHPTV began a new outdoor program and kept me on. I'm amazed I got the job, and even more amazed that I've still got it.

Windows to the Wild has taken me and the doughty NHPTV crew all over New England and the western hemisphere, from Ontario to Ecuador, and from Nicaragua to Montana. But as exciting as those places are, it's the people I've met along the way that have made the journey so rewarding—naturalists fighting to preserve essential habitat for endangered birds, cheerful fellow hikers met along the trail, and local guides who've often filled us in with the rest of the story. The crew I get to work with is an amazingly tough and resilient bunch of folks who lug heavy camera gear over all sorts of terrain in all kinds of temperatures while I'm only lugging myself.

I've been writing a weekly newspaper column since 1981, using the mantra, "Do something each week that you've never done before." Obviously, I can't afford to waste a single experience. This book is a collection of some of those columns that have had counterparts in *Windows to the Wild* episodes. I hope you enjoy them as much as I have enjoyed doing the research.

—Willem Lange
Montpelier, Vermont
May 2015

Words from the Wild

Camping on the Connecticut River

Howard Island, New Hampshire
June 2006

"Come on, Jonathon," I pleaded. "We'd better snap it up, or we're going to get really wet!" Jonathon, for his part, appeared utterly unmoved by our imminent plight. Videographers, though very fussy about damage to their precious electronics, are personally like the proverbial snapping turtle that won't let go until it thunders. Jonathon was even worse; it really *was* thundering. A regular artillery duel was developing behind my left shoulder and he appeared to have absolutely no intention of letting go or taking cover.

There was, in fact, no cover to take. Our unpitched tent lay flat on the grass of our campsite. I'd brought the Geriatric Society's big North Face mountain dome because of its capacity to easily house two campers and a pile of camera equipment. But putting it up is, as Robert Frost says, not just "Button, button, who's got the button." It requires a little experience, intelligence, and time. We were short on at least two counts, and the thunderstorm was almost upon us.

"Just give me a couple more of the Open," Jonathon said, as calm as could be. Vainly trying to match his sang-froid, I began the forty-second introduction: "Welcome to *Windows to the Wild*. I'm Willem Lange. Today we're presenting one of a series of programs that show the beauty . . ." I went all the way through it, my memory much improved by desperation.

"Good," said my tormenter. "Now once more. I'm going to start with the meadow and the river this time and pan to you. When I nod, you start."

The next few minutes are, as nineteenth-century explorers used to write, better imagined than described. But Jonathon was finally either satisfied that he had his shot or satisfied that he was about to die. We

got the tent up as the front edge of the storm reached the far edge of the field, 500 yards away. We got the waterproof fly over it and pegged down, and the cameras inside, just as it reached our side of the field. We scrambled in ourselves and then watched in awe as the deluge drummed on our waterproof wanigan and dry bags outside. Supper was out of the question for the duration, but survival seemed likely unless the big silver maple waving wildly over us chose this storm to succumb. Happy as a lark, Jonathon shot what had to be great footage of sizzling lightning strikes, thrashing trees and flying clumps of leaves, and cannon-fire thunder.

An hour later the rain had thinned to a patter on the tent, which always sounds worse than it is; so I went outside, fired up the Coleman stove (on camera, naturally; this was supposed to be a camping show), and cooked up a nice batch of pasta with cream sauce, cheese, and chunks of Spam. As we dined, it occurred to me that all that fallen water had to go somewhere, and that our canoe was beached perhaps a little too close to the river. I took a look. A good idea; the river had risen two feet, was lapping at one end of the canoe, and was charging madly past. I pulled the boat another four feet higher and stuck a stick at the water's edge to check for a further rise. There was none, so I went back up to the camp to brew some coffee.

The Connecticut River, a great wandering seam running between New Hampshire and Vermont, is probably the most underutilized recreational resource in both states. I'm not sure why unless, perhaps, it hasn't yet outlived its former reputation as "the most beautifully landscaped sewer in the Northeast." Or it could be that prospective overnight travelers on the river are daunted by the prospect of looking for a campsite on private lands, where they may not be welcome.

They needn't worry nowadays. The Connecticut River Watershed Council coordinates the efforts of several conservation organizations

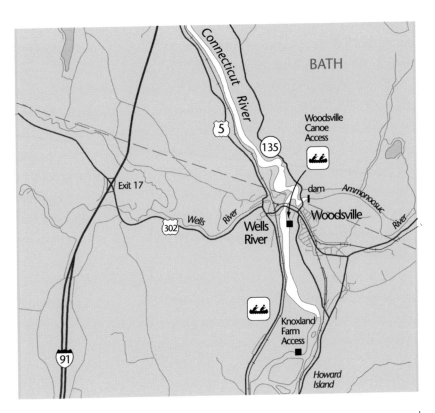

along our part of the river, and the Upper Valley Land Trust obtained the rights to campsites and now maintains them with local volunteers. Our campsite that rainy evening, on Howard Island about two miles downstream from Wells River, is monitored by one "Hemlock Pete" (his nom de guerre), a paddling enthusiast who runs a canoe and kayak business in North Haverhill. A day earlier, Pete had promised by e-mail to visit us that evening with ice cream, but the storm foiled that plan. We'll do it another time.

On a hot, muggy morning Jonathon and I loaded up our canoe just below the power dam at East Ryegate and paddled about seven easy miles, down past Wells River to Howard Island. Well, not too easy. I'd brought the big twenty-foot wood-and-canvas Old Town on the theory that it'd make a more stable platform for Jonathon's video camera. But the building thunderstorms gave us a wind right in our faces; and I'd forgotten that videographers don't paddle much. They've got a different job to do. I was feeling my age by nightfall.

We plodded along talking (again on camera) about the geology of the river, which is fascinating in its own right. Then there's its history, from the centuries of Abenaki habitation, through its exploration, the French and Indian War, and the river's subsequent development and subjugation by power dams. We battled the cranky crosscurrents at Woodsville, just as the log drivers had 100 years earlier. And we almost lost count of the birds: three kinds of swallows, blackbirds, blue herons, kingfishers, hawks, and one huge bald eagle. Still, it was a pleasure when we spotted the little sign marking our campsite.

We were never quite out of hearing of the highways on either side of the river. But the island seemed isolated and away from things. It was almost a guilty pleasure that most people know so little about this lovely river flowing right through their midst.

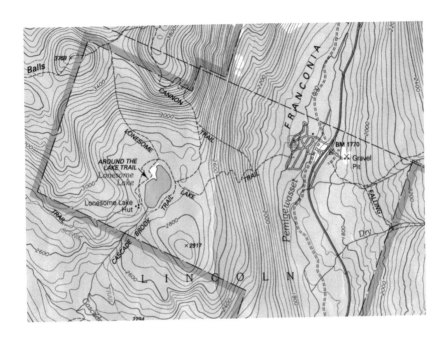

Lonesome Lake Isn't All That Lonesome

Lonesome Lake, New Hampshire
August 2006

It's likely there aren't too many places in the world as misnamed as this one. The moniker may have suited 130 years ago, when the then-well-known author W. C. Prime had a cabin here. But situated as it is, only a little more than a mile from the Franconia Notch Parkway and 900 feet above it, Lonesome Lake is one of the prime destinations in the White Mountains. On an August day like this one, cool and clear, the trail is an almost constant stream of families, young couples, and elderly climbers with hiking poles and sweatbands.

Even the appellation, "lake," is a misnomer. At twenty acres, Lonesome Lake is a small pond. But during the Victorian Era, when romantic Bostonians flocked to these mountains, all kinds of features assumed alpine proportions: lumps became mountains, shoulders became crags, and old beaver ponds attained lakehood.

A beaver bog is what it was, until the loggers came along about 100 years ago and stripped these mountainsides. They built a log dam at the outlet and raised the bog to pond status. Years later, after the log dam had rotted, someone hauled cement up here and built a concrete weir, which is now augmented courtesy of the Appalachian Mountain Club by a pressure-treated dam that keeps the water level constant. You can also see signs where beavers, still very much around, have been trying to augment it still further.

To geologists, Lonesome Lake is a glacial tarn—a shimmering sheet of water lying in a shallow basin scooped by the continental ice sheet out of two plutonic granites that formed about 160 million years ago, at the beginning of the Jurassic Period. A contact between

them runs through the pond basin: to the east, running down into the Notch, Conway granite, which is visible in the cliffs of Cannon Mountain and was the rock of the late, lamented Old Man of the Mountain; to the west and uphill, Kinsman quartz monzonite, laced with large crystals of potash feldspar. The contact between the two granites is indistinguishable to casual hikers, but one of the formations makes an important difference in this pond.

As many fishermen know, most New Hampshire waters in areas of granite bedrock are acidic by nature, and not conducive to the growth of the vegetable or larval life so important to fish species, especially native brook trout; the recent introduction of acid rain has made them even more so. Some former native trout ponds and streams have become toxic to these sensitive fish. Not so Lonesome Lake. It's surrounded by acidic black bogs with soil so low in nutrients that the insectivorous plant sundew thrives here, attracting, capturing, and digesting unwary flies. Yet the water of the pond is only mildly acidic. Its tributary stream rises high up on the Kinsman monzonite formation, and the feldspar in the formation releases calcium silicate, a buffering agent. So brook trout have thrived here since the end of the last Ice Age. In 1946 the state began stocking it with fingerlings, and it's supposed to be good fishing.

You couldn't prove it by my experience here yesterday. It was a bit sunny for fly-fishing, but I gave it a whirl. No luck over by the dam, and my back cast was threatening passing hikers anyway, so I trudged on the plank bridges over to the inlet. It was full of fingerlings and juvenile trout that scooted away like lightning at my approach; but when I waded out into the pond up to my knees, the gravel of the inlet bottom gave way to sucky, smelly mud. Once or twice I thought I was going down out of sight, just like a bad guy in a jungle movie. I got out of there, and on the way back to the hut, stepped off the boardwalk and went face first and three feet deep into a really foul-smelling black mire. The guys with me thought it was pretty funny, and snapped photos as I rinsed off in the pond back at the swimming dock, fouling the clear water all around me.

The Appalachian Mountain Club operates a forty-six-person-capacity hut up here for hikers. It advertises it as a "family hut," and the dozens of kids here bear that out. The hut crew, the usual galaxy of Ivy Leaguers, is engagingly good-humored and creative, and the cooking beats the usual undergraduate productions by a mile. Last night we had roast turkey, corn, mashed potatoes, gravy, and cranberry sauce all carried up here by the four crew members who make the trip down to the Notch every day. They also implored us to carry out every bit of trash we generate. What we don't, they have to. There are no more hidden dumps up here.

After supper last night, I felt like bed. But I knew that, whenever

I kipped out, I'd be awake six hours later. The kids were skylarking everywhere and making a lot of noise and a couple of very young ones were weeping petulantly in their bunks anyway; so I hung on till nine-thirty and then tucked in with a headlight and *High Huts of the White Mountains.*

At three o'clock in the morning I woke up and decided on a trip up the hill to the men's head. Moonlight flooded in through the screen door; I wouldn't need the headlight. I stepped out onto the porch.

A brilliant horned moon hung over the Notch and flooded Franconia Ridge and Mount Lafayette with silver light. Almost directly overhead, I saw the Milky Way for the first time in months, and realized how light-polluted the skies over the Upper Valley have become. It wasn't my usual time of night for outdoor sky viewing, and I had a really hard time identifying the unfamiliar locations of the constellations, even the Great Bear. Venus, though, hung like the landing light of an approaching airliner, just above the ridge to the east. Somebody else was on the porch, too, looking at the same sky. Neither of us spoke. Neither of us needed to.

A Notch Full of Rocks

Carter Notch, New Hampshire
October 2006

I was just congratulating myself on having negotiated several miles of really rough trail without falling once. Less than a minute later—to quote John Madden—"*Poom!*" Down I went. It was an easy fall, sort of sideways into duff and dead leaves; but a sawed-off birch trunk stuck out of the bank a couple feet off the ground, and intercepted the right side of my head on its way down.

The good news was that the trunk missed my specs; the bad news was that the result looked a little gory close-up. Jonathon, the videographer, and I still had a few "head shots" to do, and it's

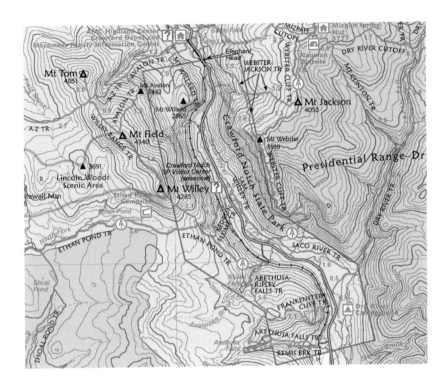

somewhat distracting to listen to a head spouting information when it's also dripping blood. So I pulled my sweatband as low as possible and we pretended we were shooting John Barrymore, who liked to be filmed in profile from his good side.

There can't be many rougher trails through the woods of New England than the Nineteen-Mile Brook Trail; I can think of only a few. Starting at the Pinkham Notch road about seven miles south of Gorham, it runs along the northeast side of Nineteen-Mile Brook and into Carter Notch. It's not much of a climb, either—only about 2,000 feet in 3.6 miles to the height of land in the notch. But underfoot, the trail slopes steeply downward from left to right, and you can't help but notice the number of trees that have given up the ghost and fallen downhill toward the brook.

Notches, they call 'em in New Hampshire. In Vermont and the American South, they're gaps—as in Lincoln, Middlebury, Appalachian, and Cumberland. In the West they're passes—as in Donner, Pioneer, and Snoqualmie. The New Hampshire name sounds rockier somehow. And this one certainly lives up to that.

You've got to wonder why in the world anybody would have ventured up into this notch in the first place. The answer is probably that he was scouting for a logging company. But if the forest in those days was anything like what it is now, it was a desperate slog—like the videos we see of intrepid explorers hacking through tropical rain forests. The trail was probably cleared later for access to a now-long-gone fire tower on nearby Carter Dome. The Forest Service, which is responsible for maintaining the trail, seems to have designated it a poor cousin; it's pretty shaggy.

On a topographic map of the trail, you can see that it follows that left-hand slope up into the increasingly tight jaws of a granite nutcracker: Carter Notch is as steep-sided as they come, and quite narrow. Looking up to my left, where a thin layer of mossy soil covered the boulders, I could see quite a few trees, even a long way from the brook bed, that also were leaning downhill. And I think I've figured out why. That whole hillside, under its cover, is a talus slope—a huge ramp of large rocks in semi-repose that have been broken off the solid mountain above by ice-wedging: a constant cycle of freezing and melting that's moving everything slowly downhill. It's the same phenomenon that recently did in the Old Man of the Mountain in Franconia Notch. So while the brook is chewing at the bedrock beneath it, the boulders are trying to overwhelm the brook.

After three miles or so, the trail—just as the guidebook had predicted—narrowed and steepened, and shortly we were at the height of land. No doubt about it; none of the usual swamps or beaver dams and open, grassy vistas; just a steep trail descending the far side one hundred feet to a glistening little tarn. Jonathon shot some views of the beetling cliffs on both sides, and down we went. The Carter Notch hut was very close by now.

We'd been given a heads-up by some hikers we'd met on the way that there were about twenty-five kids and teachers from a tony day school in Connecticut staying at the hut. Sure enough, as we tried to film the serene silence of the pond, kids' voices shrilled on the far shore. The hikers also were friends of the hut caretaker. When I asked his name, they answered, "It's her, and it's Sally." A few moments later here she came, to see who was filming her pond.

Carter Notch hut was originally a log building built in 1904 right on the edge of the pond, facing the great gray cliffs of Wildcat Ridge. In 1914 it was moved to its present location, with a view down the Wildcat River to the south. It was built of stone—naturally—though how they carried all the mortar in here I can only imagine. Nowadays it's quite a pleasant establishment, with a kitchen and dining room for forty, two bunkhouses, and a wash house. It's been run for the past ten years as a self-service hut, which means you pack in your own food and sleeping bag and use the hut's bunks and pots and pans for sleeping and cooking. The Appalachian Mountain Club, however, has seen a fifty percent drop in use over that time (in spite of sturdy caretakers like Sally, with whom Jonathon and I fell in love almost instantly). So next spring it'll revert to full service, with a full crew and prepared meals. Along with two other huts, Zealand Falls and Lonesome Lake, it'll remain open in the winter, with a caretaker, for self-service stays by skiers and snowshoers. I suspect that very few skiers will brave this trail. Those snowshoers who do make it (and Sally recommends bringing crampons, as well, for the icy slopes of the lower trail) will enjoy a spectacular view of the Ramparts, a tortured pile of angular boulders the size of bread trucks that have split from the surrounding cliffs and plunged to rest here almost beside the cabin.

It is best, before coming to Carter Notch for the night (and especially during a heavy rain or snowstorm), *not* to read Nathaniel Hawthorne's "The Ambitious Guest." You might spend a restless night, thinking about those rocks in the Rampart and listening for a rumble far overhead.

Mushing Through Maine

Kokadjo, Maine
April 2007

This is a point of view I've never before experienced. Just ahead of me, six bushy canine tails wave in the spring sun; and just ahead of each, a pair of short, erect Arctic-style ears points straight up. Beneath my poorly padded bottom, the sled runners swish, rumble, or grate as we pass from snow to ice to gravel. And just behind and above me, the musher, Steve, alternates between shouting to his dogs and sharing his and my personal histories and philosophies.

The woods on either side have been scalped several times. The trail is lined with alder saplings, with spruces poking up beyond. This may be the Great North Woods, but they've long been a working forest more than a sylvan Shangri-la. That appears to be changing a bit.

It's just six hours over here from our spot in the Connecticut Valley, and just short of 300 miles. Mother and I ran US Route 2 over here with our kids for years, headed to and from our summer jobs off the coast of Maine. I'd forgotten how straight the roads are through the woods, dipping and twisting only at each village, where a rapid in the local stream once dictated a mill and a bridge. The highway was thinly populated; the other vehicles were mostly empty paper mill chip trucks that left a sawdusty trail in the air behind them, and commuters with Maine plates, all going like bats out of Hell. I must have passed at least a hundred Arctic Cats for sale beside the road.

The old familiar names flowed past—Lancaster, Gorham, Bethel, Rumford, Mexico (a reminder of the Missouri Compromise of 1820, when Maine became a state and acquired dozens of whimsical world-atlas names), Skowhegan, Greenville. From Greenville it's another hour north over an increasingly rustic road, which the locals claim eventually turns into a cow path, then a deer trail, and finally a squirrel trail running up a tree and into a hole. I didn't go quite that far. After a quick stop to pick up a burger at the Kokadjo roadhouse, I

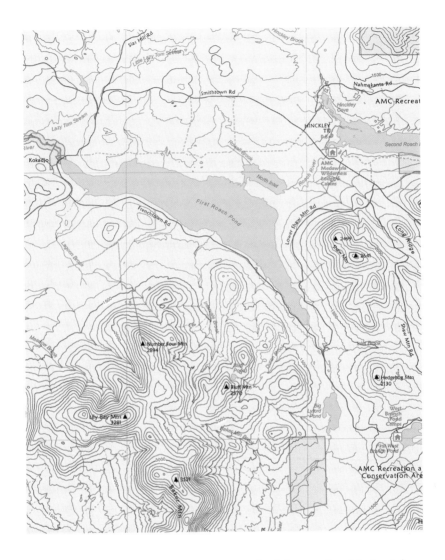

rattled six or seven miles up a spring-pocked dirt road to Medawisla, a traditional Maine sporting camp on Second Roach Pond that's recently been taken over by the Appalachian Mountain Club.

The AMC, whose White Mountain huts are pretty well filled whenever they're open, has undertaken to preserve and revive some of the old Maine camps. Besides Medawisla (Abenaki for loon), they've acquired West Branch Pond Camps and Little Lyford Pond Camps. This summer they'll probably open a fourth, at Chairback Mountain. Arranged in a string an easy day's hike, ski, or snowshoe apart, they provide the opportunity for camp-to-camp travel.

Thirty feet ahead of me, big Roy is destroying all my preconceptions of the character of a lead dog. Raised on tales of Buck, White Fang, and Sergeant Preston's famous King, I've thought of them as preternaturally sagacious, single-minded, and intuitive powerhouses. Roy is powerful, all right, but not much of a disciplinarian. When Steve shouts, "Straight on, Roy!" he does it unfailingly; but "Gee, Roy!" produces the desired right turn only about two-thirds of the time. It's almost spring here now, and tussocks of grass beside the trail have to be inspected and peed upon. Behind him on the same side, Jackson and Keno also have to make their contributions before we take off again. "That's one good thing about female dogs," says Steve. "They don't have to do that all the time." A partridge crossing the trail a hundred yards beyond a junction threatens disaster, but somehow Roy resists and leads us successfully to the right this time.

The acquisition of the sporting camps and the protection of thousands of acres of Maine forest land are part of the AMC's Maine Woods Initiative, designed to provide a little organization and muscle to the constant effort to balance logging, development, and recreational use. The Appalachian Trail passes close by here, on its tortuous way through one of the trail's most infamous sections, the 100-Mile Wilderness, which runs from Monson to the entrance of Baxter State Park. One of the club's goals is to widen the buffer zone (in which logging is not permitted) on both sides of the trail. Another is to practice sustainable forestry on a 37,000-acre tract it's acquired elsewhere in the area. The preservation of the old camps is critical. They'll attract a different clientele in years to come than they have in the past; but one look at the trout hole in the Roach River just below Medawisla, and I resolved to return myself in May or June.

Up ahead of me in the bright sunlight the six tails wag happily, but I can begin to see differences in their owner's personalities. They're harnessed side-by-side in pairs on either side of a central line. Up front, Roy and Stanzi (named after Mozart's wife) trot along, with Stanzi, the oldest dog in the team, taking her cues from the much stronger Roy. Steve says it's her last year on the long runs, which I find unbearably sad. Behind those two are Jackson and Ripley. Ripley is a lovely Siberian, brown as a deer with perfect, tiny ears. She seems to love physical contact, and is forever slipping under the central line to trot on the other side of it with Jackson, their hips moving in unison. Just in front of me are the wheel dogs, Keno and Little Bug. Little Bug is huge. Now and then he looks around at me as if to ask when I might try a few hundred yards afoot. Sorry, not today, Bug. But of all the dogs, his line is tightest; he leans on his harness with his hind feet wide apart, like a grizzly bear's. Some of the team are "rescue dogs," given up when they grew from adorable little balls of fuzz into large, demanding animals requiring lots of exercise and stimulation.

Steve, who owns and runs Song in the Woods Dogsled Adventures, is, like me, an old Outward Bound instructor, so we have lots to talk about—mostly the joy of having found our way into our respective zones of bliss, and enjoying a perfect day in the Great North Woods, along with some of the happiest and most enthusiastic companions in the world.

❦

Descent into the Maelstrom—On a Big Whoopee Cushion

Errol, New Hampshire
September 2007

"Left back! Right forward!" shouted the guide from just behind us, and the four of us with paddles, two on each side of the raft, responded with a will born of terror. The raft swung left, rose about six feet on the upstream slope of a standing wave, and plunged down the other side into a maelstrom of roaring water that could trap us. "All ahead!" he shouted, and we burst out of the hole, peering downstream for the next one. What was behind us did not matter.

Our guide and steersman, Todd Papianou, sat on the rear of the inflatable raft, a perch from which, I could not help but notice, he could be ejected at any moment. We'd been instructed on how to retrieve him, or any member of the crew, should that happen—grab the back of his life jacket, not his arms, so he'd be able to help you get him back in—but the prospect, no matter how remote, of running the rest of this river without him was very thrilling. The Rapid River is a beauty!

One of the best-kept secrets of New England whitewater rivers, the Rapid drains the famous Rangeley Lakes westward into Umbagog Lake and then into the headwaters of the Androscoggin. It lies entirely within the State of Maine; but as the saying goes, you can't get there from there—not without a lot of difficulty, at least. All the land surrounding it is in private hands—paper companies, mostly—so access is by private roads subject to closure at any time for any reason. And almost all the roads that go anywhere near the last few miles of the Rapid River, where the rapids are classic and huge, originate near Errol, New Hampshire.

Errol and the Errol Restaurant used to be known as a rest-and-refreshment stop for Montrealers headed for the Canadian Riviera—Old Orchard Beach. The restaurant featured the customary sign, *Nous parlons français,* and the proprietress, famous for her pies, was yclept, appropriately, Madame Letarte. The sign is gone now, and the restaurant's name has been changed. I hear French but infrequently, and the pies appear to be outsourced. Besides summer tourists, the big business here now is during midwinter, when dozens of long-distance snowmobilers roar into the parking lot and stomp inside, red-faced and dressed in multicolored space suits, for hot soup, fries, and mooseburgers. Just across the road, a former sporting goods emporium has morphed into an improbably huge mall of manufactured log construction, featuring everything the sportsperson could possibly want: from camouflaged compound bows to canoes and ATVs; from Carhartt overalls to hunting clothes with all the latest in camouflage fabrics; from knickknacks to gifts to moose-turd chocolate candies to deer-hunting perfume.

When I was last in Errol, I had forgotten my cane. Faced with a

three-mile hike to the head of the rapids before our raft trip down, I went into the mall looking for a replacement. Lots of walking sticks; not good substitutes for a cane. Then one of my friends came back from a foray into a distant department with a telescoping cane with a plastic head like a little ice axe and—wonder of wonders!—a halogen flashlight built into the butt end of the head. Useful, in the unlikely event I was ever benighted on the trail. And only fifteen bucks. I bought it.

Half a mile down the road, where the Androscoggin River roars under Route 26, are the office, campground, and boat storage yard of Northern Waters Outfitters, where you can sign up for almost anything on the water. Todd Papianou runs the place. A schoolteacher in North Conway during the winter, he's a big guy: a river guide, administrator, and impresario. We had a tour of the premises and drove together to a landing at the foot of Umbagog Lake. A trip across the lake on a pontoon boat, and we were at the foot of the rapids. It's a pleasant hike upstream beside the river: an old tote road. At the top, we got a

safety lecture ("Now, if you go overboard . . ."), donned helmets and life jackets, and set off downriver in three big inflatable rafts. Before the first little bit of swift water, Todd rehearsed us to see if we could tell the difference between forward and back, and how hard we could paddle. Then off we went.

The river is controlled by a series of dams with predictable, announced release schedules. We were floating on about 1,400 cubic feet per second, a "medium" release. The river is divided into a series of pitches separated by pools. The descriptions of the pitches speak of "heavy turbulence," "the pour-over near the bottom of the rapid," and "a fairly large hole on river right." Very few of these details troubled those of us in the crew; we just listened for commands from the steersman who we hoped was still there, gasped as we saw what was coming, and jammed our feet under the seats to keep from being ejected ourselves. The two young women up front were superb, in spite of being underwater for a good bit of the trip. The cameraman, too, amidships with both hands on his waterproof camera, was frequently submerged. How we never lost him, I don't know.

Halfway down, we came across Smooth Ledge, where perhaps twenty kayakers, who'd portaged their boats half a mile through the woods to get there, played in a beautiful surfing wave, trying to achieve an equilibrium where they didn't have to paddle. Most overturned instead, and popped back up a few yards downstream. One raft tried it, and threw everybody out. Todd was cool, but clearly excited; I couldn't tell whether he was shouting to hype the danger, or really was uncertain whether we'd make it through on the sunny side of the raft. Occasionally we plunged sideways into huge holes, not the way I would have wanted to do it myself. Was it accidental, as it appeared, or on purpose? It was the same feeling I had once on my first bobsled ride: This driver has decided to end it all, and this is the trip he's decided to do it! But all too soon the calm water at the foot of the Devil's Hopyard came into view, and we were done with the most fantastic four miles of whitewater I've ever run. If you've got a couple of days, you should do it, too.

A Nostalgic Trip to an Abandoned Island

Hurricane Island, Maine
October 2007

Never was there a more nearly perfect day than this one. The sun glistens on a gray-blue sea dotted with the bright colors of lobster trap buoys. The spruce-crowned islands show white granite shorelines at low tide. Overhead, the parallel contrails of Europe-bound jets point straight east by north. The wind is fresh from the southwest, the origin of the term "down east." Ravens balance on the cushion of air flowing over the bulge of the island. The day is a golden apple stolen from the gods. The locals, after we've left, will pay for it another day with fog and cold rain.

This island has been abandoned three times in its history. Overgrown, half-hidden middens of clam and mussel shells speak of a native American presence recorded in no other way. An early European

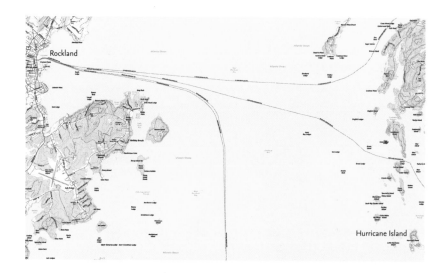

explorer spotted foxes on the islands around what is now Hurricane, and named them the Fox Islands. Later, as fishermen settled the off-shore islands, Hurricane became property. In 1870 Deborah Ginn sold it for $1,000.00 to a retired Civil War general, Davis Tillson.

From a distance the island's profile resembles a great whale. It was ground into that shape by continental ice sheets. Its beauty is breath-taking—to us who used to spend our summers here, heartbreaking. But Tillson and his partners weren't interested in its beauty. An excellent en-gineer and entrepreneur, Tillson saw a business opportunity in Hurri-cane's smooth, creamy gray granite. In fairly short order he opened quar-ries equipped with steam power and rails for transporting the stone from the quarry pit through finishing sheds to the wharf. He determined early that there was more profit in finished stone than in rough quarry blocks; so he imported master stonecutters, mostly from Italy, and before long a town of over 1,100 people had sprung up on the island.

Tillson was not a gentle master. He paid poorly, and not in cash, but in credit redeemable at only his company store. He cut the pay of workers who read the pro-labor *Rockland Opinion*, and demanded they

vote Republican. This arrangement couldn't last too long, considering that his imported Italian workers were active socialists and union organizers. At one point, frustrated by Tillson's intransigence, they even sent a delegation to Washington to visit President Hayes.

After the turn of the twentieth century, concrete began to replace granite in public construction (not fortuitously, Tillson owned limestone quarries and cement plants on the mainland). The island quarry business was flaring fitfully like a dying fire. Then in November 1914 one of the company's granite scows foundered in Rockland harbor. Two weeks later the superintendent of the works died of typhoid fever. The very next day the owners ceased production and informed the workers and their families that all operations would be permanently suspended. They could stay and starve, or take a ferry; but the ferries would be suspended in a few days, too.

Tools were left lying where they'd been dropped; tables set for the next meal waited eerily for families that would never return; pictures hung on the walls of abandoned homes. Slowly, over the next several years, a few remaining people, including a large family hired by the owners, carefully picked apart the buildings and carted the materials down to the pier for homes and other projects elsewhere. The island was silent again.

Then fifty years later, in 1964, an Outward Bound program leased the use of the island and began putting up dozens of buildings: kitchen and dining hall, offices, a huge boathouse, tents and cabins for students and staff. When Mother and I arrived here in June of 1965 with two kids, we were greeted with, "Your tent platform isn't built yet, but there's your lumber in that pile." Over the summer, as I enjoyed one of the best jobs I've ever had—seamanship and navigation, rock climbing, initiative tests, drownproofing, and the famous morning run and dip (into 45°F water)—Mother carefully built a house inside the tent. When we took down the tent in the fall, all her built-in furniture remained. She later became equipment manager, and we returned for several summers.

Now Outward Bound is abandoning the island as well. The expense of an offshore facility has become unsustainable, and the program operates fourteen other sites all up and down the East Coast. The boats and kitchen and office equipment are gone, but the huge buildings remain, already looking derelict. So Mother and I came out here yesterday, probably for the last time, to remember and to visit the quiet ghosts of the island. We arrived at low tide (as we did the first time we ever came, when Mother refused to climb the wharf ladder in a skirt until we wrapped a blanket around her). The small dog we slung fifteen feet up the side of the wharf in her flotation jacket; the sixty-five-pound Lab, too big to take up that way, wouldn't stop squirming. So I tossed her unceremoniously overboard, and after considerable thrashing, she swam eagerly ashore.

Neither Mother nor I move quite as briskly now as we did forty years ago. But that's given us the leisure to savor things as we've passed—the cavernous dining hall decked with mementoes, the quarry whose chilly water we dreaded on foggy days, the meadow and ice pond, the empty foundations, our old cabin. The cabin used to sport an anemometer atop a long, not-too-rigid staff, and on windy days the whole building vibrated like a motel bed. Those summers were among the very best of our lives. Now, the spruces and grass already are beginning to reclaim the island.

The boat is coming to pick us up. Time to pile our stuff at the head of the ladder. It's low tide again; does it ever fail? Mother says she has a great scheme for lowering the Lab into the boat. Even barely keeping afloat as I am in all these memories, I can hardly wait to see what it is.

Chipmunks, Kids, and Mountaintops

Franconia Ridge, New Hampshire
August 2008

There's a chipmunk up here on the top of Mount Lafayette. We're 5,260 feet above sea level and well above timberline in the alpine zone. This place freezes solid for several months of the year, and is often coated with a thick glaze of ice in midwinter. But there's a chipmunk up here, apparently as much at home as if he were dodging in and out of a suburban privet hedge to grab the seeds dropped from a bird feeder. There was another one on 4,807-foot Mount Moosilauke, too, when I was up there last year. How these little guys make it to the summits from timberline without attracting the fatal attentions of cruising hawks, I don't know.

There's no question about why they're on these mountaintops. More than a hundred hikers will cross this peak today, and most of them will pause here to eat a little lunch, have a drink, and toss a few treats to the chippie scurrying around their feet. He pops out without notice from various cracks and crevices and cruises the rock slabs. He never pauses to chew, but dashes off to his cache with the crumbs and nuts and M&Ms stowed in his cheeks. That must mean he plans to spend the winter here. Tonight, whatever the weather, he'll be snoozing comfortably in a hole somewhere in these ledges, while we higher forms of life retreat to our bunks in the hut below. I'll toast his health before supper and envy him his view of the sunset, the meteors, and the moonrise.

This has been a hiking week, most of it vicarious. Our older daughter flew east from the State of Washington to do a little New England hiking for a change. She planned to spend a week on the Long Trail in Vermont and then join me for three days' hiking to the Appalachian Mountain Club huts in the White Mountains. On a sunny Wednesday

morning I dropped her off at the foot of Camel's Hump, expecting to meet her a week later at the West Hartford crossing of the Appalachian Trail. Her pack seemed dauntingly heavy to me—tent, sleeping bag, stove and gas cartridges, food, maps, cooking pot, rain gear—but she obviously knew what she was doing, so I wasn't worried.

She, as well as the other two kids, got her start during the sixties on the little peaks of the eastern Adirondacks—Poke-o-Moonshine, Little Crow, the Brothers. The few photos I still have of them in those days show happy smiles, but nothing approaching what I'd call delight; so when none of them, after reaching the age of discretion, teased to keep going, I didn't push it. The same with canoeing. We all spent a month paddling the Allagash and hiking through Baxter State Park when the baby was only two; but that was the end of it. After they left home, I climbed and paddled alone or with old friends instead.

To my surprise, I began to hear about epic week-long hikes my older daughter was taking in the Cascades and along the dramatic, drift-

wood-strewn beaches of Washington. Then this spring came the news of her plans to tackle the hills of her childhood.

I thought of her all that Wednesday—How was she doing with that pack? Was there room in whatever shelter she needed? Were the water sources running all right? Sunday morning I turned on the computer to check my mail and got: *On romance mountain headed to gillispie. All fine. G* Not bad; fifty miles in four days, and "all fine" sounded good to me. By Monday evening she'd made twenty-five more miles and turned east onto the Appalachian Trail: *Here at Gifford State Park. It's quite a wonderful park. There are cabins to rent if you're down this way. Long day tomorrow, see u on W. G* (I was learning something about the miracle of texting and the contemporary use of abbreviations; you get only so many characters per message.)

In any case, that night (as the Bible describes it) the rains came, and the floods descended, and beat upon the tent—and it leaked. *Dad—change of plans. Tent leak. Will take bus to WhRiJct and meet you in norwich.*

There is, of course, no longer bus service over Route 4, so we got her on her cell phone, and Mother went to pick her up.

Now, all dried out and relieved of that onerous load, she's walking slowly behind me on the White Mountain trails and concealing beautifully the impatience she must feel at my halting, plodding pace. The cumulative effect of my multiple prostheses and fractures appears to have caught up with me. I'm seriously considering skipping dessert tonight and getting back to the gym next Monday morning. And tomorrow, instead of going on to Galehead Hut on a trail described as "the most tiring trail in the White Mountains . . . full of little bumps . . . and the trail goes over every one of them . . . ," we'll descend to Franconia Notch and climb up the other side to Lonesome Lake, a total of only a little over four miles. There's a chipmunk there, too, as I recall, who from time to time edges nervously over the threshold of the dining room door.

But for now we'll just enjoy this magnificent, memory-laden mountain. Franconia Ridge stretches away southward from the summit. Not far along it is the spot where a good friend and Outward Bound instructor was killed by lightning twenty-six years ago this month. Even closer is the spot where Guy Waterman committed suicide in February of 2000 by intentionally freezing to death. And just beneath our feet is the derelict foundation of the old Summit House, where long-ago guests of a hotel in the valley could spend the night after riding up the Bridle Path. Somebody has whimsically built a dozen or so very neat little *inuksuit* all around the top of the walls. Their spiritual implications are doubtless inscrutable to most hikers.

Haunted by memories, warmed by sun, cooled by a breeze . . . something moves by my feet. It's the little striped god of the mountaintop, wondering if we've brought anything for him.

Hang Gliding: Once Is Enough!

North Charlestown, New Hampshire
September 2008

I know, I know; I've advocated for years that everyone, especially older people, should try something new each week in order to keep body and mind functioning. But today's activity wasn't quite what I had in mind—at least for myself. I couldn't back out. I had lots of time to think about it during the drive down from Montpelier. The thoughts were dominated by a line from *Hamlet:* "...hoist with his own petard." I had to do it.

New Hampshire Public Television was recently given a grant to produce a documentary on the migration of broad-winged hawks. The good news was that we get to follow them to their wintering habitat in a preserve in Costa Rica. The bad news was that some genius at the station dreamed up the idea of demonstrating the apparently effortless flight of hawks by sending the aged host of the show (the guy who keeps recommending new experiences for old folks) up in a hang glider to experience for himself and demonstrate for the viewers the wonders of gliding on thermals and ridgeline updrafts.

I've wanted for years to do it, but recent additions to and subtractions from my undercarriage have left me unable to run fast enough to take off and, at the end of the flight, to land on my feet. "Don't bring those joints back broken," the surgeons last warned me, "because we can't fix them again." My wife and daughter, when they heard about the idea, thought it a great one, but doubted I would survive. Both of them wanted to be there to watch if I took to the skies.

"Not to worry," I assured them. "I don't have disability insurance, the station claims that my workmen's comp doesn't cover hang-gliding accidents, and the flight center will no doubt require me to sign a waiver of all claims should anything go wrong for any reason. Besides, I still

have a cord or two of wood to get in before cold weather.

"What I'll do," I said, "is interview the pilot—it's a tandem flight—and we'll talk about what's going to happen and what we're going to experience. Then we'll tape the cameras to the glider, and a videographer can go up in my place. I should be home by two." Privately, I prayed that Hurricane Gustav would speed up, turn right a smidgen, and render it impossible.

No such luck. When I pulled into Morningside Flight Park in mid-morning, the windsock was showing a light northwesterly breeze off Mount Ascutney, the few clouds overhead were beginning to flatten on their bottoms—an indication of active thermals, which hawks and gliders of all kinds rely on—and the friendliest guys in the world came out of the hangar to say hello and, by their conversation, give me to understand that I was going up. Steve Prepost, the pilot and instructor, told me he had over 3,000 flights under his belt with nary a scratch. And, contrary to my fears, the glider was on wheels—kind of like an oversized grocery cart with big nylon wings.

The video crew arrived and began taping and screwing cameras carefully to the aluminum frame of the glider. Steve and I went back to the office, where I signed everything but a blank check agreeing to hold harmless everybody in the world, no matter what. And finally we trundled the glider, behind an ATV, out to the grass airstrip.

The tug plane pulled in ahead of us, with what Steve called "the world's best tug pilot" at the controls. The towline tightened, we began to roll, and within only ten yards or so we were off the ground and climbing, bucking slightly as the ultralight pulled us through the air currents.

We climbed for quite awhile, circling in thermal updrafts whenever the tug plane found them. At about 5,000 feet the air turned hazy, wet, and decidedly chilly. "We're up in the bottom of the clouds now," Steve announced. "We don't want to go any higher because it can get pretty bumpy up in there." I concurred heartily.

Steve had warned me there'd be a jerk when the tow rope disconnected, but I forgot. When the sudden lurch occurred, I was sure we'd broken something important, and were about to break some others. But we slowed down, the flight became smoother, and we swooped around just like a huge bird, hunting for lifts. The Connecticut River valley spread out green beneath us, with Springfield and Claremont both in view.

Leonardo da Vinci, way back at the end of the fifteenth century, was the first to design a glider. Nobody knows if any of his designs ever flew until the present day, when gliding enthusiasts have made a few flights with them. The first to get a manned glider off the ground consistently was a German, Otto Lilienthal. And like da Vinci, he also pursued the ornithopter, which would flap its wings like a bird, and never could have worked. Also like his idol, he felt almost reverential about the air: "To invent an airplane is nothing. To build one is something. But to fly is everything."

I could see, as we swooped first upward and then down, slowly losing altitude and circling back toward the landing field, how some people could get mystical about soaring. But I have to admit that anxiety was closer to the surface than mysticism. We passed a hawk floating easily on a thermal, utterly undisturbed by the much larger bird beside him clutching two human beings in its talons. We crossed the river, Steve cautioning me that we would land perhaps faster than I might expect, in order to maintain control next to the ground. He circled over a ripe cornfield, lined up with the runway, and it was over. What a trip! That experience might just count for two weeks of something new.

Mother Charges Up Mount Cardigan, and Disappears

Alexandria, New Hampshire
October 2008

"Hi! Have you seen a woman in a long blue denim skirt?" I asked the question of every person and party we met as we climbed the mountain, and each had the same answer: No (with a quizzical expression that said, "Long skirt?"). After three or four of those responses, I began to feel more than a little anxious. We seemed to have lost track of Mother.

It had started innocently enough, as do most near-calamities of this type. Mother and I had driven down to the eastern foot of Mount Cardigan, at Cardigan Lodge. There we met a film crew and a couple other friends for a day of climbing and filming on the two-mile trail to High Cabin, where we'd spend the night, go on to the summit for more filming, and then hike back down. She was in charge of the cooking, and had prepared brilliantly for the shortage of water at the cabin: preboiled pasta and prebaked beef bourguignon (heat 'n' eat); frozen beans that'd be thawed by the time we got there; and a pie mix requiring no baking.

It was the Columbus Day holiday, and there must have been fifty cars in the parking lot; people, kids, and dogs coming and going everywhere. So it took a little longer than usual to find a relatively quiet spot to shoot the opening and introduction. Peter Sellers, maybe, could have pulled it off with kids playing Frisbee and strangling each other behind him, but not I. While we dithered and interviewed the manager of the lodge, Mother decided to take off before us so as not to hold us up so much when we overtook her, as we surely would.

She'd wanted very much to come along on this trip. I was delighted at the idea, but suggested that before she tackled a couple of uphill miles on the trail, she ought to walk home from church some Sunday,

which would be two miles partly uphill. She did it in a breeze; and since the crew starts and stops frequently to shoot scenery or record information, I figured she'd keep up pretty well. When she said she'd be going on ahead, my belief in never splitting the party bubbled up, but I figured it was impossible for anything to go wrong.

"How do I get there?" she asked the lodge manager. I listened as he described the route—Clark Trail, Grand Junction, Holt-Clark Cutoff, Hurricane Gap—and had the same reaction that the *Kapellmeister* in *Amadeus* has to Mozart's music: too many notes. I doubted I could follow the trails as he described them; but I have a high regard for Mother's intelligence, and an even higher regard for her oft-demonstrated resourcefulness. So I said nothing as she set out confidently up the trail alone with her brand-new L. L. Bean backpack, hiking poles, and long denim skirt—rather like a Victorian lady explorer without the petticoats.

We followed fitfully, filming as we climbed, and averaging well under a mile an hour. At the one-mile mark, we came to a spot called

Grand Junction, where several trails diverge. Luckily, we had a map with us and were able to dope our way onto the right trails. And it was just about that time I began to ask people we met coming down whether they'd seen our missing companion going up. None had.

Mount Cardigan's summit cone, only 3,155 feet in altitude, is treeless. Forest fires in 1855 burned everything in their paths, exposing the thin alpine soils to erosion, which soon left the mountain a bare, polished dome. It's essentially a granite pluton, a mass of magma pushed up from beneath the earth's crust half a billion years ago during a collision of tectonic plates. The rock is filled with feldspar megacrysts, crystalline lumps that weather more slowly than the surrounding rock and stick up slightly, vastly improving traction for hikers in slippery conditions. Great grooves in the surface mark where glaciers ground down the dome long before the trees first arrived. And the peak has a spectacular 360° view and a fire tower.

Around four o'clock we reached the cabin half a mile below the summit. My fears were realized: no Mother. On the assumption that if she was on the wrong trail, she'd reached the top, we stormed up the peak by two different trails. Nobody there; and the air literally absorbed our shouts. Below us, the woods where she probably was seemed vast and impenetrable. A pair of hikers coming up the western side of the mountain hadn't seen her, either. It was cell phone time.

Many of us who have hiked for fifty years or more disdain or derogate modern appliances like cell phones, satellite phones, and global positioning devices. If a compass was good enough for Davy Crockett, we'll take our chances with that. Thus it was amazing to me how quickly, faced with the possible loss of the most important person in the world, I overcame my puritan principles and called abjectly for help. Rob, the AMC staffer with us, reached the manager at the lodge by phone and learned that some hikers we'd queried earlier had passed the lady in the blue skirt, climbing up the right trail and "not far below the cabin." Back down the peak we flew!

We found later that, reaching Grand Junction, she'd taken the Holt Trail, described in the guide book as "very steep . . . the scramble up these ledges is much more difficult than on any other trail in this section and one of the most difficult in New England." Luckily, after scrambling half a mile or so, she'd met a trail crew, who reversed her: told her to go back to the junction and ascend by the other route. By the time she'd returned to the junction, we'd already passed; so now she was behind us, and still chugging uphill. She was delighted to see two of our party descending to take her pack and escort her to the cabin. She made supper by lantern light in the kitchen, and later brightened the dark camp with her laughter in the middle of a hard-fought Scrabble game.

A Long Night and a Long Day on Top of Maine
Millinocket, Maine
September 2009

Only eight hours ago—it seems like at least a day—I was trudging up a steep, boulder-strewn slope half-hidden in mist and blowing clouds. I knew I was close to the summit of the mountain, but the cairns seemed to go on forever. Then I met a young man coming down. His boxy yellow articulated foam sleeping mattress, his large pack, and his odor marked him as a long-distance hiker. His face wore a slightly dazed smile, and he seemed to want to share something. "Is it possible," I asked him, "that you've just finished a very, very long walk?"

Yes, he had. His trail name was Sailor J, he was from Baltimore, and he'd started the Appalachian Trail at Springer Mountain, Georgia, on April 3. "What'll you do now?" I asked.

The notion seemed to startle him. "Well, first I've got to figure out how to get down this mountain. They tell me all the trails are rough. Then I guess I'll hang around Maine for a few days, and then, I'm not sure." I offered him a handful of gorp, and we parted. Shortly afterward I reached the cairn at the summit that has ended thousands of hikes like Sailor J's.

Some time after dark this evening I drove my truck down the eight-mile dirt road from Roaring Brook Campground to the Baxter State Park gatehouse. At the posted speed limit of twenty miles an hour, it seemed a long way. I could hardly believe that only twenty-three years ago some friends and I skied up that road in February, hauling pulks loaded with winter gear, and the next day climbed up onto the mountain. Not tonight. I doubted that when I got out of the truck I'd be able even to walk.

Still, the jet-black sky, unstained by any earthly light, beckoned. So at one opening in the canopy of trees, I stopped, turned everything

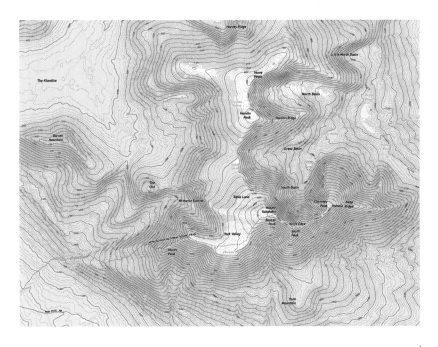

off, and got out. Jupiter hung in the south like a great landing light; the band of the Milky Way stretched all across the sky that I could see. I climbed stiffly back in and putted down to the gate, where two young rangers checked me out. (The park is tightly managed, and the staff knows where each visitor is, or ought to be, at all times.)

Now, an hour later, the night sky is washed in the glare of a hundred parking lot security lights, the aircraft warning lights of the smokestack of the Millinocket paper mill, and the luminescence of a McDonald's. I've checked into an Econo Lodge rather than dodge moose and deer all night. Dawn, the desk clerk, has given me a room with a "pool view" (translation: no outside window), and I can't get cell phone service. If I could, I'd call Mother to tell her I'm off the mountain, safe, uninjured, bathed, and bedded; also that I'm having trouble getting around the room because I can't lift my feet high enough to climb up over the edge of the carpet.

Mount Katahdin (Thoreau, who climbed it in the 1840s, spelled it "Ktaadn") rears up dramatically from an infinity of spruce, pine, fir, and birch. Its Wabanaki name means "the big one." It's surrounded by 200,000-acre Baxter State Park. Former Governor Percival Baxter, heir to a Portland fortune and a genuine character, had loved brook trout fishing in the area as a child, and grew to feel that the magnificent peak and its forests should be rescued from constant cycles of logging and preserved as a wildlife sanctuary. He tried fruitlessly for years to get the legislature to set aside money for the purpose. Frustrated, he began to buy the land himself in bits and pieces.

Often he was able to buy a section for a very low price by, for example, allowing the seller a few more rounds of logging on the property before turning it over. Eventually Baxter had put together a patchwork quilt of land, which he gave to the people of Maine under a deed of gift with strict conditions: If human activity threatens the wild nature of the land or any of its native denizens, it is to be halted till the impact has been negated. And if any abuses are not mitigated or halted, ownership reverts to Baxter's heirs. This explains the strict rules governing the park's use.

Our crew spent the first night in the bunkhouse at Roaring Brook Campground, planning to climb the mountain the next day and spend the second night at another bunkhouse higher up, in the spectacular setting of Chimney Pond on the floor of the cirque called the Great Basin. But that first night was one that will live in infamy. I hadn't remembered that the bunks were plywood, so had brought no sleeping pad; the cooking gear was too small to make my supper; the woodstove heated the place to at least 90°F; and one of the guys had a very loud Cheyne-Stokes snore that would have kept everyone else awake in the best of conditions. It was no problem to roll out at five in the morning, grumpy and unrefreshed, pack silently in the dark, and start up the 3.3-mile trail to Chimney Pond. We dropped our overnight gear in the bunkhouse there, and tackled the mountain.

I'd forgotten something else: There's no easy trail up or down Mount Katahdin. Carved by mountain glaciers that left long boulder trains for miles around, shattered into rubble by freezing in postglacial times, and festooned with rock slides, the mountainsides are obstacle courses—for an old guy, at least; the kids around us swarmed up and down it like orangutans. At the top, on which I hadn't stood since 1971, I felt little exhilaration, but instead the same concern voiced by Sailor J: How in the world am I going to get down this thing? Luckily, the rest of the crew stayed with me all the way back to Chimney Pond, and one of them even added my pack to his own as I clambered slowly down— backwards on almost all the steepest, most threatening pitches.

On the way I swore that if there was any gas at all in the tank when I got back to Chimney Pond, I'd keep going and forego the pleasures of another night of plywood, snoring, and starvation. And so I did. . . .

A Presidential Traverse
Madison Spring Hut, White Mountains, New Hampshire
August 2011

The wind roared around the hut here all night; but like the Biblical house built upon the rock, it fell not. With its thick stone walls, it didn't even tremble. But when I got up a little while ago, just after dawn, and peered out the window into the maw of a thick cloud moving about fifty miles an hour, I'll admit I did tremble a bit at the prospect of launching out into such a williwaw. Then I reflected that the hut is located right at timberline—less than 100 feet higher on either side, the balsam and spruce krummholz gives way to tundra—and that, descending, I'd be out of the worst of it in no time.

The four of us in our crew rode the Mount Washington Cog Railway a couple of days ago, experiencing for the first time the power and speed of one of the new biodiesel locomotives. The train let us off about 1,200 feet below the summit, where the Westside Trail ducks under the trestle. We made our way leisurely to the Lakes of the Clouds

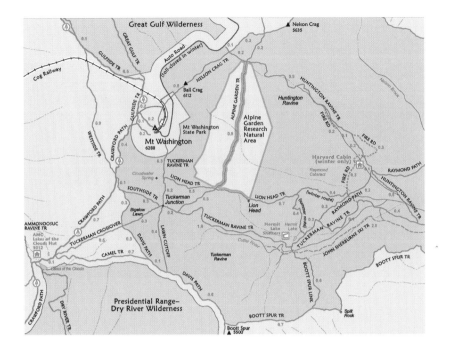

Hut, perched boldly on the saddle between Mounts Washington and Monroe. Early as we were, we were able to pick out good bunks, which was a relief to me; I'm usually so late arriving that, like the Devil, I take the hindmost (in the case of the huts, the top bunk of three or four), and then experience anxious moments climbing down in the pitch dark on my much-repaired legs to go to the washroom during the night.

We left our packs on our bunks to claim them and went off to climb Monroe, a sharp-pointed little peak with an unbeatable view of the Dry River Wilderness to the south and east. Then back to the hut for a preprandial toot and the usual sumptuous supper. The hut was booked fully for the night—it holds ninety—so it was a hive of activity: an extended Midwestern family group ranging in age from six to seventy-nine; a group of thirty-nine kids winding up a month of environmental studies and camping; the usual handful of romantic

duos getting away from Boston for a vigorous few days of hiking; and a clutch of Appalachian Trail thru-hikers, who don't pay, and sleep in the basement. They don't dine with the regular guests, either, but sit nearby on a bench, ready to help with camp chores in exchange for leftovers after meals. The seven-member "croo" served us all homemade bread, meatless lasagna, green salad, juice and coffee, and dessert, all with the usual rough, jovial aplomb.

Some of the eight Appalachian Mountain Club huts have been around a long time. A rough stone shelter was built in 1888 where the Madison Spring Hut stands today. Lakes of the Clouds is the descendant of an emergency shelter built after two hikers died on Mount Washington in a summer storm in 1900. All but one are on state or federal land, and operate under permits as a "public service." Since the permits must be renewed from time to time, the Club has been at some pains to mitigate the huts' negative effects on the fragile mountain environment. Thus the electricity for lighting, refrigeration, and communications is generated by solar panels, small wind turbines, and in one case, water power. There are no paper napkins in the dining rooms (what are your grubby old hiking shorts for anyway?), and no

wastebaskets anywhere; what you carry in, you carry out. There's bot-
tled gas, flown in by helicopter, for cooking. Barrels of sewage from the
toilets are flown out the same way. It's as lightly as several hundred pe-
destrians per night can possibly tread upon the Earth without leaving
indelible wounds.

I lay awake for a couple of hours in the hut at Lakes, worrying
about the next day's hike to Madison Hut. Fifty-five years ago, on a
brisk September day, some friends and I skipped across the Presidential Range like young chamoix, but those days, and that ability, are now
long gone. I was genuinely concerned about making it across, as well as
wondering what the options were if I couldn't. We left at eight o'clock,
after breakfast.

Washington loomed above us, 1.4 miles away and 1,200 feet higher,
studded with its myriad towers and buildings. Again we skirted it and
ducked under the railway trestle. The Gulfside Trail stretched before
us, visible for miles as it looped around Mount Clay, then Mount Jef-
ferson, and finally the great bulk of Mount Adams, seeming almost im-
possibly distant. But off we went. The die was cast. Steve, who's worked
on the mountain, showed us where in October 1990 a Cessna with
three Texans flew just a whisker too low across the Washington-Clay
col in thick cloud cover, hit one of the stone cairns marking the trail,
and tumbled over the edge into the Great Gulf.

Thunderstorms had been forecast, but didn't materialize. The wind
was west and southwest, gusting to at least sixty miles per hour. It carried the sound of the steam whistle and the smell of smoke all the way
up from the base station of the cog railway, where one of the coal-fired
old-timers was just setting out. Not a bad day at all, with only 6.8 miles
to cover on a relatively level trail. The kids working at the huts sometimes jog it round-trip just to make social calls on days off.

It's a young person's trail, no doubt about that. As I teetered gin-
gerly from boulder to boulder, placing my cane carefully to maintain

a two-point contact with the ground, young people skipped past in both directions, full of cheery greetings, as if they were auditioning for *The Sound of Music*. Two fathers from Connecticut slogged uncomfortably toward us, several hundred yards behind their bored and unsympathetic sons. I soldiered on around Mount Adams as my shadow slowly lengthened before me; and finally, a few hundred feet below, lay the hut.

I quaffed quarts of Madison Spring's ice water to ward off cramps, rinsed and hung out my sweaty duds to dry, practically had to wrestle a Canadian woman to hang onto my floor-level bunk, and was off early to bed as the storm clouds blew in. Now I'm about to start down the mountain before breakfast, betting it'll be clear and sunny before I get to the bottom.

A New Year's Day (Climbing) Party

Mount Moosilauke, New Hampshire
January 2012

New Year's Day started for me at what my son, during his time in the military, used to call "O-dark in the morning." Ken showed up in our backyard a little bit after six-thirty having walked over from his house just down the road. I pulled the truck out of the garage, we loaded up, and were off to Bradford, Vermont, where we met Gary, Don, and Eric. Consolidating into two trucks, we crossed into New Hampshire and followed Gary's lead over back roads to Glencliff. Our sixth member was there—Steve Giordani, a doughty, intrepid, and indefatigable videographer from New Hampshire Public Television. On our trips into the bushes, Steve is everywhere: running ahead to catch us approaching, silently filming our conversations and water breaks, lugging heavy equipment over impossible terrain. I swear he'd continue shooting if a shark had him by the sacrum.

Our goal today was the 4,802-foot summit of Mount Moosilauke in Benton. It's somehow become a tradition among Upper Valley hikers to trek up the mountain every New Year's Day, no matter what the conditions. This makes the adventure a little hairy at times; but this New Year's forecast was for above-freezing temperatures, a south wind, and clear skies slowly giving way late in the day to clouds and rain. If ever I was going to do it—considering the ever-quickening march of time—this was the year.

In past years, First Night business has kept me up late and pretty tired; but this New Year's Eve I was done by seven o'clock. I had time to pack and sleep before the five o'clock alarm clock got things going the next morning. Mother had put up a lovely trail lunch and left it on my desk after supper.

I'd been up Moosilauke dozens of times, once even on another New Year's, in 1969, in a howling whiteout and blizzard; but never since then in winter, and never by the Glencliff Trail. To say that the prospect of this climb dominated my thoughts for over a week before would be an understatement. Forty-three years older, thirty-two pounds heavier, and much patched by the orthopedic wizards at the Hitchcock Clinic, I was a bit doubtful of the outcome. So, I sensed, were the friends to whom I mentioned it—as well as my family. Not exactly a cheering section.

The big question for me was what I was going to wear on my feet. On our 1969 climb—a Dartmouth Outward Bound break-in hike— we wore snowshoes, and were very glad of it, because we had to bivouac on the mountain that night, and used the 'shoes to dig ourselves a sleeping platform big enough for us all. But we wouldn't need them this year, Gary assured me, because there'd be so many faster climbers ahead of us who'd pack down the trail. Eric, another New Year's regular, corroborated that. But I would need some really good ice creepers, they warned, because there was often ice underfoot the whole way up. Great! So I asked around, and a friend offered me the loan of a pair of adjustable crampons. I gladly accepted, but neglected to fit them to my boots until it was too late to look for an alternative. They were too small. So I fell back on my only alternative, a pair of "Get-a-Grips" that I got for Christmas some years ago: designed primarily for old people going for the newspaper or navigating supermarket parking lots. I crossed my fingers, hoped for the best, and decided not to mention it. Perhaps no one would notice.

Clambering over difficult terrain in a party is a constant flashing back and forth between internal concerns (pain, anxiety, fatigue) and camaraderie. Don and Gary, who've climbed together often, call themselves the Persistent Plodders, which I found encouraging; I'm pretty slow lately. Eric seems to have assumed an almost formal role (he's a doctor, and knows what's going on with my legs) as my protector and sheepdog—something I deeply appreciate. After we climbed beyond the bare ice of Glencliff and began to tackle the steeper mixture of ice and snow above, he stayed right behind me, warning of imminent slips of creepers from my heel and pulling them back up.

The AMC guidebook mentions a half-mile-long steep stretch beginning at 2.5 miles and ending at the ridge of the mountain, where the Glencliff Trail merges with the much gentler Carriage Road that once provided access to the long-extinct Summit House hotel. It was steep, alright! With the stone steps that normally make it easier now coated with flow ice, it demanded the introspection I mentioned. I could feel the lactic acid building up in my quadriceps, hear my breath a bit labored—as the legs fail, the lungs find it easier to keep up—and realized for sure that, whatever prospect that steep slope ahead presented, I was going to make it. We did, and I became extroverted again.

An easy, spectacular mile on gleaming crystalline snow above tim-

berline took us up the gently rising ridge to the ruined foundation of the Summit House on top. The south wind was a bit brisk, blowing dense patches of mist up and over the ridge. The giants of northern New England were visible—Washington, Lafayette, Mansfield. We lingered for a bit and walked back down to the trail junction, where Gary and Don uncorked their traditional small bottles of champagne and we toasted our success. Other parties lingering there also cheerfully shared the moment. We shot photos and video. The bonhomie was palpable. Then Eric and I, for fear of the danger to me of descending that sloping ice on the trail below, strode off down the Carriage Road: a little more than a mile longer than the other route, but much safer. We emerged from the woods just after dark.

That was yesterday. The difficulty I had getting out of my truck at home and crossing the yard from the garage prompted me to stand my cane beside the bed when I turned in. Good thing I did; it's the first three or four steps after any rest or sitting that are the most exciting. After that, I can begin to think again of what's next. A volcano in Nicaragua in February, I believe—even higher than Moosilauke. At least I shouldn't need those miserable creepers!

Camping with the Scouts—Again

Camp Carpenter, New Hampshire
February 2012

I'd almost forgotten how much fun it used to be to go overnight camping in cold weather with a bunch of other boys whom I knew only
through our membership in a Boy Scout troop. But all around me here
have been the sounds and sights of happy campers: hardwood fires
blazing in stone rings, boys seated in circles passing around hot pots
of macaroni and cheese, and the whack of axes splitting wood. Friday
evening, when we made the rounds of various Scout camps scattered
through the woods here at Camp Carpenter, everybody we talked to
seemed delighted to be here.

To satisfy a truth-in-reporting requirement, I must admit that all of
us here have dodged a major weather bullet. The forecast for early this
weekend promised an arctic cold front and clear skies. So I brought my

husky four-season tent, the -20°F sleeping bag, polyfleece boot liners, and several layers of fleece and down. But the front has stalled west of us, held back by a slow-moving warmer system to the east, so we've been basking in temperatures around 20°F, and I didn't need snow-shoes to stamp out a circle in the snow for my tent.

The weekend campout is called a Klondike Derby, and borrows some mythology from the Klondike Gold Rush of 1898, in which dog sleds and an ability to operate successfully in very cold weather were at a premium. So each competing patrol—there are over 200 boys here, with their adult leaders—has built a sled to carry its required gear. Instead of a line of dogs to pull it, the boys do it, with one of them riding or running at the back of the sled to steer and stabilize it.

Camp Carpenter comprises a little over 200 acres surrounding Long Pond, just east of Interstate 93 and south of Manchester. It boasts a large dining hall and function room, cabins, lean-tos (called "Adiron-dacks" in New Hampshire), camping and activity areas, and a Scouting museum. When it was first laid out, half a century ago, its setting was quiet. But the city's metastasizing suburbs and the growth of its air-port now provide a low, constant background roar; and when large, Miami-bound jets take off, our film crew has to stop recording. From my tent, I can look through an oak grove and the slingshot target range to the back side of a row of generic condominiums. If the boys notice, they don't give any sign of it. They're just as excited about what they're doing as if they really were somewhere in the bush near Dawson or Whitehorse.

The Scout troops began to pull into camp after school Friday, and continued to arrive well after dark, setting up in their assigned camp-sites. The flickering fires reminded me of the line from Julia Ward Howe's famous marching hymn: "I have seen Him in the watchfires of a hundred circling camps. . . ." Big tarps went up over picnic tables and stoves; piles of split firewood went up beside fire pits; and tents

popped up in every halfway-level dry spot. During the evening, inspection teams of older Scouters visited the camps with checklists of required items—first aid kits, hats, gloves or mittens, jackknives—and awarded or deducted points. Taps was at ten o'clock.

I was up just before six o'clock and was making breakfast on the Coleman stove—scrambled eggs, cheese, bacon, coffee, and sweet rolls—when the film crew showed up with their camera batteries recharged after a night indoors with electrical outlets. We dined, washed up, packed away the tent, and abluted before a cannon went off at eight to announce the start of the Derby. The patrols of Scouts began dragging their sleds around the pond on a woods road, stopping at stations along the way to perform outdoor skills tests on which they were graded. Because of the lack of snow, almost all the sleds were mounted on wheels, some with great originality and others with obvious last-minute desperation. One Senior patrol opted to stick with just skis and carry their sled on their shoulders like a coffin. It worked better than anyone expected; they won their class.

We followed a patrol named Dynamite, whose cheer (required for entry to each activity site) was, *"Boom! Dynamite!"* They were first required to lash together a sawhorse, set a heavy log upon it, saw off a two-inch-thick section, and bore a hole through that to make a wheel—all of this within twenty minutes. But their sawhorse was a bit too limber, so they lost a few points. They went on to Fire-Building (flint-and-steel; they did beautifully), Knots and Lashings, Map and Compass, Obstacle Course, Ice Rescue, and several others, ending up with a Citizenship quiz. Through it all, they were judged on Organization and Delegation, Problem-Solving, and Leadership. They gained points if the judges at each site could pick out the leader without asking; then each leader was judged on his performance. Dynamite's leader was a very impressive kid named Jacob, clearly in charge and respected. It occurred to me that if I were a prospective employer, college admissions officer, or military recruiter, this event would be ideal for checking out candidates.

There was another quality, rarely overt, but thoroughly in the grain of the organization. I can best express it by what kept running through my mind: "Toto, I've a feeling we're not in Vermont anymore." This was the good old-fashioned God-and-Country conservatism that I knew in Boy Scouts myself sixty years ago, before I went off to school and became a smarty-pants liberal questioning every assumption. There was authority here—and unquestioning acceptance of it—that we don't see much in general society these days. I heard and saw no cell phones. The boys were consistently called boys. When I opened my food box in the company of some leaders and lightly mentioned that my wife had sneaked in a one-ounce bottle of whiskey, everybody jumped back as if it were an angry rattlesnake. I hid it. Only a churl would attempt to disturb or disrupt in any way this great weekend of learning practical and social skills that will last for life. It was good to recall how much fun it used to be to thrash around in the winter woods with a bunch of other boys.

A Trail Too Far, and Far Too Steep

Lonesome Lake Hut, New Hampshire
August 2012

Don Vandenburgh is a lively member of Tom Brokaw's greatest generation. He recalls clearly the Battle of the Bulge, in which he used his earlier winter camping experience to survive frigid nights. While his buddies huddled in the backs of trucks and suffered frostbitten feet, Don dug holes in the snow, rolled out his insulating pad, passed the nights in his sleeping bag, and woke up in the morning ready to go.

After the war, Don and his late wife raised a passel of kids whom they took hiking as often as possible. An engineer by profession, Don was also a Scout leader and family trip organizer. His son Rich recalls early hikes: "[T]he knapsack I was given ended at about the back of my knees. I have little doubt, however, that this caused me any concern and am sure that I was as excited as my siblings in preparing for the next of many trips back to the mountains. The sense of excitement in preparing for the next trip is still palpable."

Don was here at the AMC hut this morning with two of his sons, Doug and Rich, for an on-camera interview. Don's eighty-nine now, and not as strong on the trail as he once was; but the three of them climbed the 950 feet and 1.4 miles from Lafayette Campground and got here by eight o'clock. They carried Don's huge old packbasket and his iconic sheath knife, made from a German bayonet, with circular bits of plastic from a German tank periscope threaded onto it for a handle. The "boys" (Doug just returned from a hike to Everest Base Camp; Rich is an attorney) seem as excited by these artifacts as the old man is proud of them. Don and I both got our starts in the Adirondacks. We shared stories of Mount Marcy in winter (the can of soup his mother packed for him froze solid; the frozen strawberries I packed never did thaw out) and old-fashioned camping equipment—shelter-half pup tents, coated nylon ponchos, and blanket pins. It was great to talk with somebody who remembers all that antique equipment and hair-shirt hiking.

A couple of years ago, wanting to celebrate their father's life in the mountains, the family offered to help underwrite the replacement of the dilapidated Kinsman Pond Shelter, a three-sided lean-to two miles and 1,200 feet above Lonesome Lake. Cooperative projects always take a bit of bureaucratic harrumphing, but eventually the idea was approved. The job was given to John Nininger, owner of The Vermont Wooden House Company, who's built some pretty fantastic, beautifully fitted log homes. John was here today, too, to show off his handiwork. Doug and Rich both helped him with the actual construction, and remember warmly that at the end of almost every day's work, the helicopter that brought up the logs also took them back to their cars.

How I wished for that helicopter today! After a filming session with Don down by the beach at Lonesome Lake, the rest of us hiked up to take a look at the shelter. As we hiked, I kept thinking I recognized the trail. Then I remembered I'd hiked it over fifteen years ago, on the way up and down North Kinsman Mountain, and thinking at the time, "Wow! This is really steep and rocky!" Little did I know how time would further steepen this miserable trail and thicken the treacherous moss on its smooth slabs of rock. After a while I gave up looking over my shoulder to speculate how in the world I was going to get back down afterward.

Sally Manikian, the AMC's director of backcountry sites and facilities, met us at the shelter, so we had a full house. We chatted for the cameras, dined variously on raw carrots, cucumber, Skor bars, and cashews. The shelter, with its generous ground clearance and wide eaves, should last at least three generations. We peered underneath the floor where we'd been told a board with old Don's handprints was secreted. And finally it was time to retreat. Doug and Rich took off first, to pick up their father at Lonesome Lake, and escort him slowly back down the trail to Lafayette Place. I left next, because everybody

else always catches up with me, and I hate to hold them up.

The Fishin' Jimmy Trail, as it's called, is definitely not an old person's trail. Even the Appalachian Trail thru-hikers we met on it today were marveling at the change in their daily mileage since entering the White Mountains. "My usual days were twenty to twenty-five miles till I got here," one complained. "Now I'm down to five." I sympathized, and teetered downward—backwards in some places too steep to risk a stumble facing forward.

Steve, the videographer, passed me first, carrying his gear and headed for the parking lot three miles down, where he'd check his mail and set up his next day's schedule. Then the beauteous Sally bounded past like an impala, with her dog right behind her. She made as if to linger for moral support, but I waved her regretfully on. Then Phil, the producer, went by, promising to wait for me at the hut. Finally I was alone, except for the occasional group headed up or down. I trudged on, wondering—as I'm sure hundreds of others have before me—whether this was the best place they could possibly have put this awful trail. Surely there must be a better way.

Around three o'clock, I spotted the gleam of the hut's roof through the trees. As I came into view of the back steps, I spotted a crowd of people gazing up the trail at me with rapt attention. I straightened up against the pain and strode toward them. Then I realized they were looking over my shoulder. I turned around, and saw behind me the biggest bull moose I've ever seen in New England. He was Alaskan!— at least five feet across the antlers—and quietly munching birch twigs.

It's about three-thirty now, time to start down. A mile and a half to go, 950 feet down. Then home. A piece of cake, and the end of another romantic day on our rustic little Hollywood set.

Hiking with Tom and Atticus

Passaconaway Campground, New Hampshire
September 2012

It's a little past three in the afternoon, and bright and sunny here about twenty miles east of Lincoln on the famous Kancamagus Highway. A perfect day: I got to climb a new (albeit small) mountain; the temperatures were mild at last; my little magic carpet Tacoma, which will take me home, is running like a top; I have a nice dry shirt to change into; and I've made a couple of new friends. Can it get better?

First, the highway. It's named after one of the last leaders of the Penacook Confederacy of Native Americans. Almost everybody living in New England has driven it at one time or another. It probably appears to most visitors to be passing through forest primeval. This is an illusion; the whole area was logged extensively—even rapaciously— and burned during the days of New Hampshire logging camps and railroads. It's now National Forest land, and continues to be logged, but under the supervision of the Forest Service. The road itself is one of those 1930s-era engineering masterpieces, connecting two dead-end roads that extended into the wilderness toward each other from either end. It opened officially in 1959.

The highway heads east out of Lincoln, past the entrance to the Loon Mountain Ski Resort, and follows the east branch and then the Hancock branch of the Pemigewasset River upstream to a height of land at 2,855-foot-high Kancamagus Pass, which is not always open during a hard winter. Cyclists like to have their photographs taken—for good reason—beside the sign at the top of the pass. On the eastern slope, the road follows the infant Swift River, which tumbles toward the Saco at Conway. To the south, the Sandwich Range of the White Mountains squeezes it up against the river. That's where we hiked today, about halfway between the ends of the highway.

I've discovered in the past two years that I perspire pretty heavily while hiking uphill, and have learned the hard way a few of the perils of dehydration: loss of equilibrium, slower hiking, and irrational decision-making. So I've begun carrying extra water, in spite of its added weight, and keeping fresh shirts and bandanas in my truck for afterward. My favorite trainer at the gym has just suggested mixing the water half-and-half with electrolyte replacement; that'll be my next experiment. I also have a catalog in my head of all the McDonald's I'll pass, whether traveling to Pittsburg, New Hampshire, Bar Harbor or even Millinocket, Maine (where I learned one late evening, exhausted from a day up and down Katahdin, that it was the only open restaurant in town). Thus, on the early-morning drive to trailhead rendezvous I load up on carbohydrates and, after a sweaty day, make my first stop on the way home at the nearest oasis with large strawberry shakes.

Our primary purpose today was not hiking or experimenting, however, as much as it was meeting two people I've wanted to meet for some time. It's difficult to know how to introduce them—normally

you'd say, "a man and his dog"—but the relationship between these two is not like that at all.

Atticus M. Finch and Tom Ryan are pals, one Irish, gregarious, and chatty, the other self-contained and silent. The history of their coming into each other's lives is too complicated to detail here. For the full story, get Tom's book, *Following Atticus*. You'll probably continue on by adding the address of his blog to your web browser's bookmarks page. It's a lively one.

About fifteen years ago—Tom is sparing with dates and real names—Tom was a one-man band, publishing a muckraking weekly newspaper in Newburyport named *The Undertoad*, after the warning given the infant Garp by his mother: "Beware the *Undertoad!*" He'd alienated most of the town's old guard and power players, not to mention the local police, who often dined in unfriendly groups next to his breakfast table at his favorite diner and eventually even stole his trash from the curb in a search for something damning. He was single and lonely, in spite of many friends in town, and as he says, looking for something he was missing, something new, something next. He was also badly out of shape, around 300 pounds, and found it hard to walk very far.

Chance, as well as a rash, imprudent impulse brought him an elderly miniature schnauzer named Max. He and Tom began walking . . . and walking . . . and eventually even hiking. But all too soon Max succumbed to seizures and old age. Again, this is abbreviated; but soon afterward a breeder in Louisiana sold Tom a miniature schnauzer puppy whom he named Atticus M. Finch, after one of his favorite heroes in literature. Atticus, it developed, loves hiking mountains, and once on top of each, sighs, sits down, and gazes Zenlike at the view. Tom writes of him, "He is Frodo Baggins; he is Don Quixote; he is Huck Finn. He is every unlikely hero who ever took a step out the door and found himself swept up in adventure."

Atticus is ten now, and hopped up the mountain today perhaps more thoughtfully than he did some years ago. He reminded me—and it brings tears to my eyes just now as I write it—of our dog now long in her grave who joyfully climbed everything with me from Mount Monadnock to Moosilauke, just as quietly as Atticus today, and whose interactions with other hikers were, like his, most lively when she wondered what they were having for lunch on the mountain that day.

There's much more: hundreds of winter-and-summer climbs for cancer research and animal hospitals, for example. And another book coming out soon. Tom, the consummate Irishman, hints tantalizingly at its contents, but won't say what they are. I, the consummate Dutchman, am about to head over the pass with predictable haste to my customary strawberry shake.

A Busy Week Ends with a Loop

Montpelier, Vermont
October 2012

"You want to try a loop?" Peter asked from the seat behind me. I glanced quickly at the altimeter on the control panel in front of me. About 4,000 feet; light overcast; heading into a southerly wind. All this registered in much less time than it takes to tell it.

"Sure," I answered, hoping my voice betrayed no hesitation. A second later the horizon in the windscreen became suddenly an unbroken carpet of autumn colors as we dove. "Pickin' up a little speed," said Peter.

Then he must have pulled back hard on the stick, because I weighed more than 600 pounds. The carpet of color became a blank screen of gray, and I weighed nothing. Then I was hanging in my harness, and nothing visual made any sense. But my mind was racing: He hasn't got enough momentum to get up over the top, I fantasized, and we're

going to spin! I think I reached for the buckle of my four-point safety harness, the first step in getting ready to pop the canopy, roll out, pull the rip cord on my parachute, and pray for the best. But in the half-second it took to think all that, the horizon reappeared—upside down!—I was squashed back into my seat, and we were floating softly along again as we had been, with only the sound of the wind around the canopy. My breakfast returned to its proper location.

"How'd you like that?" Peter asked.

"Whoa-ho! That was something!"

"You want to do another one?"

"I think that, in deference to my stomach, I'd rather not." I've mildly regretted that response ever since. How often do you get to do a loop in a sailplane over Franconia Notch?

This New Hampshire Public Television outdoor show we're filming madly as the shooting season draws to a close has made it much easier for me to fulfill my commitment to do something new each week.

Some weeks I pile up enough new things to last me the following month.

This one began in a Holiday Inn in Concord, New Hampshire. Not very outdoorsy, I know; but Mother and I were there for the premiere of NHPTV's latest special—*Bird Tales*—about migratory songbirds that travel from North America to the Caribbean and beyond. There were questions from the audience afterward (always interesting), supper with the crew, and finally off to our room. Next morning at breakfast, the Chinese couple at the neighboring table asked if we knew where they'd find leaves at their peak of color. In the old days, I'd have pretended I knew and sagely guided them up into Franconia Notch or onto the Kancamagus Highway. Mother, however, suggested Google. I added, "Foliage New Hampshire." A minute later they looked up from their iPad, nodded effusively and said, "Yes, yes, thank you! Got it!"

After a rest day, I took off the following morning to do something that, far from new, could easily get old: the seven-hour drive from Montpelier to Bar Harbor, cutting across the geographic grain of New England and in traffic almost the whole way. But it was worth it. We poked around Mount Desert with Michael Good, the proprietor of Down East Nature and Birding Tours, with whom we're hoping to travel to Cuba this winter.

Birding with Michael was definitely—embarrassingly—new. Woods that I would have passed without a second glance were, to him, alive with tiny songbirds: a large flock of yellow-rumped warblers on their way south, chickadees, nuthatches; on the beach: eiders, scoters, sandpipers, yellowlegs, loons, a great blue heron, cormorants, and bald eagles—many of them within a few hundred feet of busy traffic. Not only could he spot and identify birds I wouldn't have known were even there, but he could hear 'em, too. He must have parabolic eardrums.

All too soon we had to tear ourselves away for a five-hour drive to Franconia. The westering sun made every spot of dirt on my windshield an opaque smear. Stopping for gas, I squeegeed the inside of it, which made life a lot easier—not to mention less deadly. The crew were long behind me. I had a burger at the local restaurant, checked into Franconia Lodge, and slept like the dead.

Morning, the day of our sailplane flight, broke with a thin layer of frost on the truck and a thick layer of fog everywhere. But by eight-thirty, the ground crew at the Franconia Soaring airport was warming up the towplane, a 1956 Cessna reconnaissance craft whose camouflage paint barely covered its French Air Force markings. FAA regulations require that if a loop in a glider is contemplated, all aboard must wear a parachute. I got my instructions and climbed stiffly into the narrow seat up front. The film crew fastened little video cameras here and there on the glider, the towplane hooked its line to our nose, and we were off, jouncing down the grass runway, a legacy of the Second World War. The jouncing stopped, and we were up, climbing toward Mount Lafayette.

We dropped the line somewhere above 5,000 feet, and were on our own. Low clouds streamed over Cannon Mountain and ran down its sides. With a glide ratio of 38:1, the sailplane felt (to me, at least) just like a regular light plane, but a lot quieter—nothing but wind noise past the canopy. Then Peter popped the question I'd been half-dreading. And that's where we came in.

North of the Notches
Happy Corner, New Hampshire
October 2012

It was an easy afternoon's drive over here yesterday from Montpelier, so I took the time to stop at McDonald's in Lancaster for a senior coffee and a couple of apple tarts to go. Then, where US Route 3 reached Indian Stream, I turned left and stopped for a few moments at the quiet little cemetery a few rods north. I often check the grave, up next to the back fence, of Minik, a Polar Eskimo brought south by Rover Peary. After an unhappy, checkered career, Minik died in a New Hampshire logging camp during the 1918 Spanish flu epidemic. His name is misspelled "Mene" on his tiny stone, but various visitors over the years have found it and brought little presents to leave near it—a miniature *inukshuk* (an Inuit cairn), a bit of walrus ivory, small flowers.

Happy Corner sits astride Route 3 a few miles north of Pittsburg Village, on the way to the remote border station near Fourth Connecticut Lake. Pittsburg, at a little less than 300 square miles, is the largest town in New England, yet only 869 people called it home in 2010—about three souls per square mile. Only one main road crosses it, but it's laced with logging roads and recreational vehicle tracks. In the 1830s, because of disputes over where the international border with Canada was located, and since both nations involved claimed this area, the residents finally revolted and formed their own short-lived Independent Republic of Indian Stream.

North of the corner, the road is dubbed Moose Alley. Hundreds of cars in season slowly cruise the highway with cameras ready, in search of at least one of them—much to the frustration of the drivers of logging trucks and trailers. (Signs warn against stopping on the roadway.) The corner is dominated by three establishments: Mountain View Cabins (our destination for the night), the barnlike Happy Corner Café, and the supermarket-sized Young's Store. The same family owns 'em all. Perry Stream, once one of the contenders for recognition as the Canadian border, flows past on its way to First Connecticut Lake, and in logging days this was a prominent junction.

One family in Perry Stream Crossing, as it was then called, had a Victrola, so their home became an informal Saturday evening gathering place. One thing led to others, and soon the place assumed the name Happy Corner. It lives today on the income from logging, tourists, moose- and leaf-peepers, fishermen, hunters, and—most of all—snowmobilers. This week, it's grouse hunters: they're everywhere, with orange vests and hats and dog whistles around their necks. You might think this the home of rugged rangers of the forests. Well, they're rugged all right; but almost nobody who lives here goes anywhere for

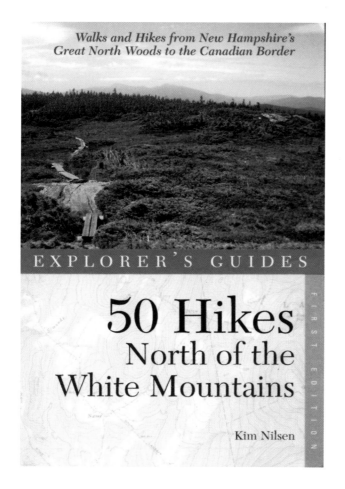

Walks and Hikes from New Hampshire's
Great North Woods to the Canadian Border

EXPLORER'S GUIDES

50 Hikes
North of the
White Mountains

Kim Nilsen

business or pleasure without the aid of an internal combustion engine. The ambient background noise, winter and summer, is engine exhaust.

I generally arrive at these northern venues ahead of the rest of the crew, who drive from Durham after a day's work. So I checked into the cabin and picked out a good bed, got ready for my usual evening toot, and realized to my horror that I had brought with me not one drop of the water of life. I gazed appraisingly across the road at Young's Store; it looked to me as though it might have an oasis within it—a watering hole, as it were. I was right; and a few minutes later was lounging in a

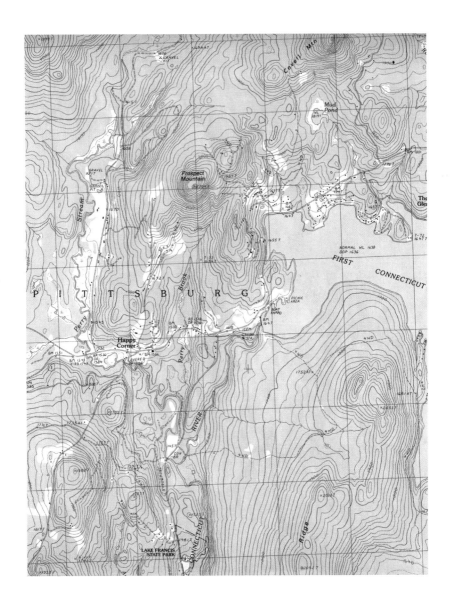

white plastic lawn chair on the front porch of the cabin as the darkness and evening cold settled down around an increasingly happy corner of northern New Hampshire. After a while, the crew showed up, along with the "winner" of this year's New Hampshire Public Television auction of "A Day with the Crew."

We're here, north of the White Mountain notches, to talk and walk with a prodigious hiker and writer named Kim Nilsen, who's recently published a guidebook titled *Fifty Hikes North of the White Mountains*. Nilsen fell in love with this country years ago. The high peaks of the Whites get all the attention, and hikers swarm over them all through the year. But here, just a few miles north, are hundreds of square miles of forests, laced with wild streams and punctuated by mountains up to about 3,700 feet in elevation. Nilsen, who likes his hiking less crowded than it is in the high peaks, set out some years ago to establish marked trails all through this neck of the woods. He also writes as glowingly about this country as Leif Erikson once rhapsodized about Greenland.

His major achievement has been the 165-mile Cohos Trail, which wanders north from Crawford Notch all the way to Fourth Connecticut Lake, a quiet beaver bog that backs up to the Canadian border. The trail is still being improved, with more lean-to shelters planned, but it's blazed and cleared the whole way. At the border, it connects with a Canadian trail system that takes hikers even farther north. But he's inspired other trails—the fifty of the book title—and helped a crew of volunteers to cut and maintain them. They may lack the majesty of the bare tundra peaks just to the south, but they have their steep rocky spots, too, where avalanches over the years have tumbled boulders down the mountainsides. And because of the relatively unbroken habitat, wetlands, and lack of crowds, they're much richer in wildlife.

We started our day with a two-mile hike along the upper Connecticut River, here just a roaring, plunging stream between high banks. Some years ago, Nilsen discovered a forgotten waterfall here. No one who lived in the local area knew about it; but piles of shattered rocks piled along the banks attest to long-ago blasting by the river drivers to clear the flume for logs. It was a beautiful hike, with the rich aroma of fresh balsam thick in the air. In the afternoon, we took a half-hour hike up Prospect Mountain, perfectly named for its view—from the Whites in the south, and Maine in the east, to the Canadian border mountains in the north, with a broad-trailed hawk and kestrels overhead. Just east of us rose 3,383-foot Mount Magalloway, which I think I'll take another crack at next month during deer season.

In any case, I'm sure to be returning to Happy Corner.

Fishing with Alfred
Lyme Center, New Hampshire
January 2013

As the old calendar in front of me reaches the end of its life and is lifted off the desk, to reveal the new one waiting beneath, the focus of my imagination shifts from the recent past to the future. The rifles in the gun cabinet seem to take on the glow of an Old Masters painting in deep tones of American walnut and blued steel. When my wife, years ago, gave me the shell of the cabinet, I customized the interior to contain two enthusiasms. So, while the rifles and shotgun settle down for another ten months' wait, the fishing rods, in their own assigned slots to the right of them, begin to assume a new importance. We're ready, they suggest impatiently, whenever you are. It won't be long, I answer; we'll be fishing again with Alfred in about five months. That, in turn, reminds me of my fairly recent introduction to Alfred.

It arrived in an unprepossessing little package—clearly a CD or

DVD—and I confess it took me a couple of weeks to get to it. Finally, in an idle moment, I opened the mailer, stuck the enclosed disk—a DVD—into the computer, and settled back with a cup of coffee.

A man in New England wool hunting togs stands at the edge of a thicket a rod or so from the camera. Speaking in the purest New Hampshire accent I've heard in decades, he introduces himself—Alfred is his name—and hopes the viewer will enjoy the following video footage of wildlife he's taken around his home and property.

I expected to see chickadees or northern cardinals at a feeder, probably a minute or two of deer on the far side of a field, and maybe some distant shots of nervous loons diving out of sight. But within a minute, I was hooked. There were loons, all right, up close, three of them in full cry—the microphone on Alfred's tiny video camera is surprisingly good—apparently engaging in a courtship display. The male thrashed his feet and wings till practically his whole body, with its pure white breast distended, rose vertically out of the water time after time. The other two cruised in circles around the display, calling in that unmistakable yodel I remember so well from early-season fishing trips in northern Maine and New Hampshire.

As the loons faded away, a beautiful bobcat, on the *qui vive* and taking nothing for granted, zigzagged slowly through the woods toward Alfred's camera and a smear of blood in late-winter snow. Then followed a porcupine, close-up, chomping busily on low-growing leaves. Right away, I sent the DVD to New Hampshire Public Television, with a note: This is a guy we've got to meet!

If you think Downton Abbey's driveway is long, you haven't seen Alfred's. He lives in the woods at the end of a dirt road east of Lyme Center, New Hampshire. But he has electricity and Internet; we got in touch and set up a date to meet and do some fishing. Scheduling a shoot with two busy videographers, a boat, a canoe, four life jackets, paddles and oars, fishing gear, and camera equipment is about as complicated as D-Day. Early the appointed morning, we all met at the Dartmouth Skiway and set off for a nearby pond to look for loons, moose, and fish.

We drove for about half an hour, the last half-mile over one of the worst roads in New Hampshire—left that way, probably, to protect the pond. Alfred's truck was old, and his skiff even older. I liked him at first sight. Compact, muscular, neatly bearded, and contained, he handled the boats with the assurance of decades of experience. Modestly, he demurred at being filmed for the program. "Are you kidding?" I said. "This is New Hampshire Public Television, and you've got the most nearly perfect New Hampshire accent I've ever heard! You gotta be in it."

It rapidly becomes obvious, when you set out to film wildlife, how much patience and skill it takes to be successful. We saw no moose and two or three loons, who let us get within fifty yards, and caught one small bass. Later, at Alfred's house, we did get shots of a black bear.

Alfred lives on the north edge of relatively unbroken forest and has an advantage in the bear department; one of his neighbors, Ben Kilham, raises and releases orphaned or injured bears, who tend to hang around. Alfred knows their habits, and sometimes sits for hours in a blind near his house to film them.

When I got home that evening, I played Alfred's DVD again, and was even more amazed than I was at first. He moves so silently, or not at all, through the woods that he sees more than most of us even suspect: a merganser with three chicks paddling madly behind, imitating her every move; two bear cubs playing on a downed dead tree like daredevil kids on a jungle gym; a bull moose nearing the rut, unsure whether to run or contest the passage; a close-up of a white-faced hornets' nest, what Robert Frost calls "the pupil of a loaded gun"; a family of otters sliding happily through pond weed. A red fox, bothered by the noise of the wind, hunts through tall grass and finally pounces successfully upon some fat rodent, which it bears away to its kids. A coyote, its fur fluffy against the winter, walks toward the camera, which is perched behind a deer carcass in the snow. Suddenly the coyote spots what's going on, and leaps away in the most comical fashion, like a running pronghorn, stopping twice to look quizzically over its shoulder before it disappears.

I went back a second time, and we had pretty much the same poor luck fishing as on the first. But I took the guideboat, which makes fishing as comfortable as sitting in an armchair—and you sit at each end, twelve feet apart, not in each other's way, chatting as easily as in a drawing room. Today, just as I was gazing at the rods in the cabinet and dreaming of the perfect moment of this year's first fish striking, I got this e-mail: "When we fish [the pond] next spring we will catch some nice bass!" I hate to tell him, but as lovely as it is to catch some nice bass, it almost doesn't matter.

The Recovering Woods of Maine
100-Mile Wilderness, Maine
March 2013

I'm not quite sure where we are, though any old native would say, "You're in Maine, ya damn fool!" My friend Put and I drove east from Greenville for several miles two days ago, past the airport with a lovely old DC-3 parked at the terminal, then on through a hundred log jobs, on a road as iced as a bobsled run, to a large parking lot where an Appalachian Mountain Club snowmobile shuttle picks up the gear of people coming to stay at its lodges. They pick up people, too: those who'd rather ride than ski the several miles to camp.

Yesterday, Shannon, our irrepressible guide, mentioned that we were skiing through the Bowdoin College East Grant, which put us in Township T7 R9. See what I mean? I have almost no idea where we are. She pointed to a very natural-looking bit of northern forest: "the School Lot," set aside for the location of the school in the very unlikely event the township is ever incorporated. "That lot probably hasn't been logged for 100 years," she said. It looked it.

The Appalachian Mountain Club, during the past few years, has acquired about 60,000 acres of former timber company land in northern Maine. This, along with the Appalachian Trail property, has protected an unbroken corridor of conservation land all the way through the famous 100-Mile-Woods to Mount Katahdin. In addition, the club has purchased and renovated three old sporting camps, one of them originally a nineteenth-century loggers' camp, and is promoting camp-to-camp skiing, hiking, and mountain biking. I'm accustomed to the White Mountain hut system—Madison, Greenleaf, Lakes of the Clouds—but was advised by Rob Burbank, the AMC's Public Affairs Director, to say "lodge-to-lodge" when mentioning these accommodations on-camera.

I must admit he has a point. The White Mountain huts don't have hot water, showers, or saunas. These lodges do; and it's quite a treat, after a day trudging through the snowy woods, to doff everything, take a leisurely turn through the sweat lodge and the showers, and then don fresh duds (ferried in by the trusty and cheerful snow machine drivers) for supper in the dining room.

It's a long way over here from the Connecticut Valley; you've really got to want to be here to drive that far. Put lives in Lyme Center. I drove down from Montpelier early the other morning, praying for clear roads, and met him at the P&H Truck Stop in Wells River. Our rendezvous was for five-thirty in the morning, but Put was for many years a Vermont dairy farmer, and retains that perverse rural notion that the earliest riser is the most virtuous person around. So I got there at five-twenty, and as I climbed out of my truck, he strolled out of the restaurant as if he'd been there for some time. I was damned if I'd ask. We loaded his skis, poles, and packs into my truck, and were off— north to St. Johnsbury, east on Route 2, with the usual obligatory stop at McDonald's in Lancaster, to Skowhegan; north from Skowhegan to

Greenville a little before our eleven o'clock meeting time with the camera crew. A quick lunch in town at Auntie M's, and we were off for an afternoon's skiing and shooting.

It quickly became evident that the AMC's so-called Maine Woods Initiative is pretty popular. A gang of happy Vermonters from around Morrisville was just coming out of the woods as we arrived, and another larger one, from Massachusetts, was heading in. The dining room would be full that evening, with barbecued chicken in the offing.

Those skiers who choose to be transported all or partway to the lodge ride in a fiberglass Sno-Coach. It's not like the snow coaches in Glacier Park, and not for the claustrophobic or anxious. It's a tight fit for three adults; I had to practice various approaches in order to fold myself up enough to get in and out. It seems suspiciously high off the ground and top-heavy, like an old stagecoach, and if you let your imagination loose, you can easily create a calamity in your mind. But it whisks riders in jouncing, rattling semi-comfort at up to thirty miles an hour. We were able to get all our scenic and skiing shots in time to hit the sauna at the men's hour of four-thirty. One diehard woman sat defiantly in a corner till sheer numbers of Y-chromosomes drove her out at last.

One reason the AMC was able to afford the purchase of these forest lands is probably that they've been pretty well scalped by decades of corporate logging. Percival Baxter, who purchased all of what's now Baxter State Park just north of here (but never spent a dime he didn't have to), did it that way: offering peanuts for logged-off property with an eye to what it would again become. Put and I—he's even older than I am—will never see it, but a few decades of rest, combined with sustainable harvests, should see it lose its desolate look and regain much of its natural beauty. Meanwhile, the surrounding granite peaks, with Katahdin's snowy crown dominating the horizon, are reminders of what this was when Henry Thoreau came through and wrote *The Maine Woods.*

We spent that first night at Little Lyford Pond Camps, where Shannon and I had fished a couple of summers ago for native brook trout. The next day we all set out for Gorman Chairback Camps, which have been extensively renovated, and a beautiful new lodge constructed, with funds provided largely by the Gorman family of L. L. Bean. The trails were beautifully groomed by the busy snowmobile squad, and the air temperature just about freezing. Lovely!

You can't take your own bottle to Chairback because of liquor license restrictions, so you do what everybody did during Prohibition: you drink in ill-disguised privacy. One large group of skiers—professors and scientists—had gotten into camp fairly early, spent the late afternoon in a cabin, and arrived for supper in a very merry condition. They jovially invited me to teach them the waltz interlude to "Logger Lover." I declined. Tomorrow was going to be another long drive.

Devil's Gulch in the Heart of Eden

Eden, Vermont
July 2013

"Close to the center of Devil's Gulch there is the slightly scattered and lightly bleached skeleton of a young bull moose." (with apologies to Ernest Hemingway)

Smack in the middle of a July heat wave from Hell, I'm in Eden. The maples and beeches, in full green leaf, provide at least a bit of relief from the furnace of the apocalyptic sun, but the deer flies are pretty thick, and keep us hopping. I see that one managed to drill me on my right forearm a few minutes ago; a rivulet of blood runs down from the hole she left. I can't help but smile when I reflect that the first thing she did when she scissored through my skin was dribble into my arm a little of her saliva, which contains an anticoagulant. My blood already

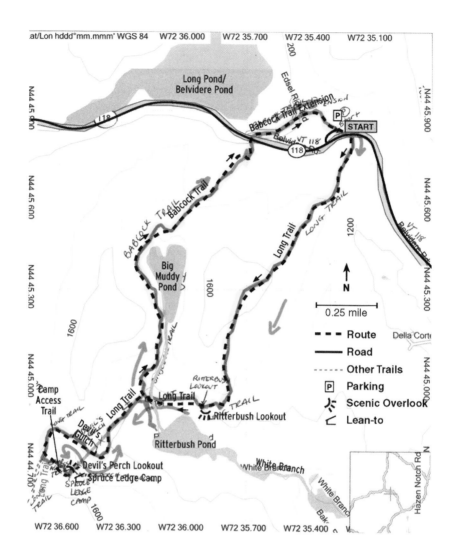

contains a prescribed anticoagulant. She must have thought she'd hit the Spindletop gusher.

The town of Eden lies quietly (about 1,150 citizens) in Lamoille County in north-central Vermont, about thirty miles from the Canadian border. The Long Trail passes through here, though it's used less at this latitude than where it follows the ridge of the Green Mountains. In

1781 the infant State of Vermont—then still the Vermont Republic—granted the land to the near-mythical Seth Warner and the men of his regiment in recognition of their service in the Revolution.

Hilly, rocky, and a long way from anywhere else, the land was of little value for farming. The person who named it Eden obviously had a strong sense of irony. He also knew his Bible; the Gihon River, which drains from the town of Eden and joins the Lamoille at Johnson, is one of the rivers that flows from the Garden of Eden in Genesis. It's also possible, I suppose, that an early settler, steeped in Scripture and wandering the forest, came upon this ravine and, awed by its huge tumbled boulders and thick coat of moss everywhere, relegated it to Satan.

Gulch is a uniquely American word, derived, as are so many Americanisms, from Anglo-Saxon Middle English. It once meant " to swallow greedily." It's much more common in the West—Helena, Montana, for instance, was originally Last Chance Gulch—and a not unusual way to get rid of people you didn't like was "dry-gulching," shooting them from the cliffs as they passed through. Along with *ravine, canyon, gorge,* and *gully,* it can carry sinister implications. During prescientific days, when calamitous natural events were usually attributed to unhappiness among the gods, clefts in the earth were often invested with gloom, mystery, and danger.

One of the first books I read as a child was *The Bears of Blue River,* by Charles Major. The protagonist, a frontier lad named Balser Brent, kills several bears, one in just about each chapter. Naturally, he was my hero. The bear that really captivated me—still does, when I consider how vividly I recall it almost seventy-five years later—was the so-called Fire Bear, which glowed at night, terrorizing the settlers, and caused the death, within three months, of anyone who saw it.

Balser, armed with a mystical charm, tracks it to The Black Gully: "The conformation of the rocks composing its precipitous sides was grotesque in the extreme; and the overhanging trees, thickly covered with vines, cast so deep a shadow upon the ravine that even at midday its dark recesses bore a cast of gloom like that of night untimely fallen." Naturally, Balser manages to kill the Fire Bear, at night when it's glowing fiercely, but at the climax of the hunt loses his friend Polly, whose torch ignites natural gas rising from the floor of the Black Gully. The bear is later found to have made his bed in the gully in bioluminescent fungi—foxfire—which accounts for his eerie appearance. I was delighted, back in 1996, to find a paperback reprint edition of the original, which can still raise the hair on the back of my neck when I hear the cry of poor Polly riding down the winter wind.

It's a pretty easy two-mile hike in here on the Long Trail from Vermont Route 118, a few miles northwest of the junction at Eden. The New Hampshire Public Television crew and I are walking with Jennifer Roberts, author of a new Appalachian Mountain Club guidebook, *Best Day Hikes in Vermont,* along with her sister and nephew. The book describes sixty hikes. Jen's done 'em all, from Haystack Mountain on the Massachusetts border to Brousseau Mountain up in Norton. I've tried a few—it would take more years than I have left to go through the whole book—and have found her descriptions accurate. She throws in little tidbits to liven things up: the now-defunct general store in Norton, for instance, built smack on the border with a door at each end, so Canadians and Yanks alike could shop there.

You enter Devil's Gulch by climbing a wooden scaling ladder and slipping beneath a huge tabular boulder leaning up against the cliff. The rock here is metamorphic schist, with an almost-vertical cleavage plane. After the gulch was formed, probably by a combination of glacier and stream, the overhanging side began collapsing, leaving the gully floor a jumble of huge boulders. Halfway through, clambering over and threading through obstructions, we came upon the skeleton—not large; antler nubs on the skull. It evoked a number of questions and somber scenarios.

Beyond the Gulch and at the end of a gradual, steady climb, we arrived at a Green Mountain Club shelter with a lookout to Belvidere Mountain and its shuttered asbestos mine. I remember climbing Belvidere in February of 1989 with veterans of the original Tenth Mountain Division, who in February of 1945 captured Mount Belvedere in Italy in a costly battle. All of them around seventy years old, they struggled in the deep snow; but at least, as one observed, there were no Germans shooting at them.

We hiked back through the Gulch and past the somber skeleton, Hemingway's epilogue humming in my mind: *No one has explained what the moose was seeking in that gulch.*

Mysteries of Dogtown

Dogtown, Cape Ann, Massachusetts
August 2013

If, during the summer, you get online and Google-Earth "Dogtown, Mass.," the satellite view will focus on a nude, brown smear in the middle of a great patch of green trees. If you back away a little, you'll see that the green forest is surrounded by a thickly urban environment. Not like Baltimore, say, or downtown Boston, but a solid mass of roads, factories, and businesses, and residential areas stretching all the way to the sea on one side and back toward Essex and Beverly on the other.

The brown area is the municipal compost pile for the city of Gloucester. Just beyond it, at the entrance to a wide trail into the woods, is the beginning of Dogtown Commons. And thereon hang many tales, many mysteries, and paintings.

If you'd been able to scan this view from space about 9,000 years ago, you'd have seen what the first immigrants must have found: a tortured, hilly glacial moraine surrounded by salt water, rising from sea level to about 200 feet, studded with drumlins, bogs, and swamps, and littered almost everywhere with boulder trains and erratics the size of houses. Those first immigrants, the Agawams, did not long survive the exotic diseases introduced by fifteenth-century Europeans.

Those later arrivals settled by the sea in 1623, named their port after Gloucester in the old country, and set about harvesting the abundant cod just off shore. The Gloucester Fisherman's Memorial, whose famous bronze statue is familiar to us all, is surrounded by bronze plaques bearing the names of the thousands of Gloucester men known to have been lost at sea.

Port towns were vulnerable to attack from the sea. Some Gloucester residents moved inland, into these uplands now known as Dogtown, when the town opened plots here for settlement in what's known as "commons": Each person with a title had equal access to the resources of the land held in common. The abundant forests were subsequently cut down for shipbuilding and firewood, and the cleared land used for farming and pasturage. Dozens of overgrown cellar holes of that vanished community still pock the landscape like the ruins of bejungled Mayan temples, giving Dogtown the aura of an archeological site.

The origin of its name is probably an example of after-the-fact myth-making. The accepted story is that the great number of widows living in the woods—widowed by war or the sea—kept dogs for protection; and that after the women's deaths, the dogs roamed free, adding a pervasive implicit threat to these hinterlands. That sounds apocryphal. It's more likely that as the community declined—it's long been extinct—its inhabitants were considered increasingly marginal and "strange," and the common American pejorative was applied to them and their neighborhood. By the time the last resident, a former slave named Cornelius Finson, was removed in 1839, half-starved and frostbitten, from the cellar where he lived, Dogtown had become a wilderness of haunted ruins.

The New Hampshire Public Television crew and I came here today to film the place and hear some stories about it from its two leading experts: Elyssa East and Ted Tarr. Elyssa is a Manhattan-based writer whose 2009 book, *Dogtown—Death and Enchantment in a New England Ghost Town*, explores Dogtown's 300 years of interaction with the town of Gloucester. Ted is a seventy-eight-year-old Korean War veteran, a former Rockport selectman, a descendant of one of Cape Ann's earliest settlers, and a frequent guide for hikers of Dogtown. Elyssa would guide us during the morning, Ted in the afternoon.

Both made singular entrances. When Elyssa climbed out of the car of a friend who'd brought her to the Dogtown parking lot, she was seven months pregnant, but declared herself—in spite of others' advice—ready for the hike. Ted showed up in a desert-tan Hummer the size of a Sherman tank with a safari platform on the roof, and climbed out as if that were perfectly normal.

Elyssa was originally attracted to Dogtown by the paintings of Marsden Hartley, one of the first American modernists. Hartley had found relief from deep depression by painting the fantastic boulders of Dogtown; Elyssa set out to find them, and fell in love with the mystery of the place. Could a particular landscape, she wondered, affect the consciousness of its inhabitants; or were the inhabitants already people who would be attracted there? We hiked Dogtown Road, the former thoroughfare of the settlement, visiting cellar holes, while Elyssa described who'd lived in the long-vanished tiny houses that once sat atop the piled boulders. I'd seen a few pictures of Dogtown, but they were all taken before the reforestation of the place. What had once been expansive views with huge erratics in the middle distance were now intimate encounters in thick groves of oak and beech.

Elyssa left us before noon, escorted by one of our interns (it's easy

to get lost here, even if you know the place). Ted took over, leading with an upright, almost military step over increasingly rocky paths. We passed a boulder inscribed with the death date of "Jas. Merry," who went to his pasture to wrestle his bull and did not survive. Ted led us to the Boulder Trail, one of Dogtown's roads leading through a series of erratics engraved with messages of an inspirational (and vaguely capitalistic) nature. Roger Babson, a local millionaire, professional predictor of market trends, and founder of Babson College, hired unemployed stonemasons during the Great Depression and set them to work carving: INITIATIVE; IF WORK STOPS VALUES DECAY; SPIRITUAL POWER; and the like. I had my photo taken next to INTELLIGENCE. Then we slowly wound our way back to the parking lot, said our goodbyes and thanks, and plunged back into the maelstrom of rush-hour Gloucester. But like Elyssa and Ted, I've found I can't get the place out of my mind.

Hiking in the Dark

Mount Willard, Crawford Notch, New Hampshire
August 2013

I half-turned and spoke to the tall man a few steps behind me on the trail. "Randy, there are three really sharp short spruce stubs sticking out on your right side, just about eye level. The first one's the worst."

"Thank you," he said. Raising his right hand, the one with the hiking pole in it, he felt in the air ahead of his face for the branches, found them, and inclined his body away as he passed. His dog, in his left hand, who'd paused as he'd felt his partner's hesitation, started up again.

Acting as Randy's early-warning system feels pleasant and familiar. Both my parents were deaf from about the age of ten, victims of spinal meningitis that destroyed their auditory nerves. They had no sensation of sound and no natural balance in the dark. So from our childhood my sister and I acted as their ears—on the telephone, at the auto repair shop, at meetings where the speakers didn't sign and had no interpreters. (My worst moment occurred when, at Bishop Peabody's retirement banquet, the bishop referred to "intercontinental ballistic missiles." Try signing that in a hurry.) It wasn't always a pleasant office, but it was always a necessary one when they asked, so it became second nature.

Many blind people have some sense whether they're in the dark or the light; Randy doesn't. In 1989, about a year after he graduated from the University of New Hampshire in electrical engineering, he began suddenly to lose his vision, to a still-unidentified neurological disease. Within a few weeks he'd lost his right eye, and had tunnel vision in the other. Eleven years later the lights went out entirely; he remembers vividly the last glimpses he had of the sighted world.

My sister and I used to talk about which of the two senses—sight and hearing—we'd choose to lose, if we had to. Naturally, we chose hearing. Our father could drive, which for a missionary to the deaf was a blessing. Except for not hearing, there wasn't anything they couldn't do. But in those days before the communication systems now common, they were almost completely cut off from hearing society. Both of them could speak normally (though I gave up after several years trying to correct Dad's pronunciation of his car as "Pon-tay-ic"), and my mother could read lips pretty well. But the nervous reactions of hearing people to their disability—they were called, at the high end, "deaf mutes," and at the other, "dummies"—separated them ineluctably from everyone but their friends in the "deaf world." No wonder there were monthly meetings of the various fraternal organizations of the deaf; it was their main chance to feel normal. When television came along, about the time we kids were in our teens, Dad used to say, "You want to know what it feels like to see everything going on and not quite understand it? Try watching television with the sound turned off." It was a good lesson for us, and we began to wonder if being cut off from

seeing the world wouldn't be preferable to being cut off from people and their conversation.

Randy is definitely not cut off from conversation. I doubt if he's ever quiet for more than a few seconds, at least on the trail. It's probable he needs the give and take in order to locate who's where and what's happening. Two years after he lost his sight, the same disease attacked his cerebellum, and soon he was in a wheelchair, suffering from migraines

and vertigo. About the same time, his first guide dog died unexpectedly of cancer. It couldn't have gotten much worse.

That could have been the end of it. But with persistence and some experimental therapy, he got out of the wheelchair, started walking with a new dog, kept up his season tickets to Patriots' games, and even began to tackle small New Hampshire mountains with a girlfriend. In 2010 he proposed to Tracy on the Welch-Dickey Loop Trail near Waterville Valley; they were married in October. About that time, he conceived a plan to hike all forty-eight White Mountain 4,000-footers.

Mount Willard rises to only 2,800 feet, and its trail, a former carriage road, is only 1.6 miles and pretty easy, but it's ideal for our purposes today: to hike with Randy and his dog, the Mighty Quinn; to film their partnership on the rocky trails and slippery stream crossings; to talk with Randy about how he fixed on the goal of climbing the forty-eight; and to hear about his charitable organization, 2020 Vision Quest, dedicated to improving the lives of folks with disabilities. Plus there's the matter of the tattoo on his shoulder, celebrating his status as the New England Patriots Fan of the Year in 2001. That was a good year to be Fan of the Year; the Patriots won the Super Bowl, and Randy got to go with the team to the White House to meet the President.

Hiking with Randy, I find myself occasionally trying the exercise my father recommended with the television audio, but this time by closing my eyes. Even with both hiking poles, two steps forward is clearly death-defying, and I can only imagine how Randy manages to feel and teeter his way across rocky, slippery brook beds. Yet as we chat today, I learn that he's managed to climb all the 4,000-footers in winter (easier, he says, than summer because the rough spots are snowed under), and tomorrow he'll tackle Mount Isolation, a fifteen-mile round trip, along with Quinn and a group of friends. That'll leave him just two shy of the summer forty-eight.

At the overlook near the top of Mount Willard, he said, "That's Mount Jackson across the Notch. Take my hand—I'll point my finger—and trace the skyline with it, will you?" I ran his pointing finger up the left skyline to the summit, over the peak and down the rough southern ridge. He smiled as if he could really see it; and perhaps he can. His shins may be a bloody mess from bashing trailside rocks, but his face shines with a joy that I almost envy.

The Warrior Hikers
Smarts Mountain, New Hampshire
September 2013

As I write, a group of friends has just three days ago finished hiking the Appalachian Trail by reaching the summit of Mount Katahdin in northern Maine. The following day they starred at the annual Trails End Festival in Millinocket, and I presume they're all on their way home by now. The news of their successful completion of the trail, as well as photos of the Millinocket event, are here at my desk, just a click of the mouse away.

It's ironic that we should be able to get news and photos of distant events within minutes of their occurrence, when the events themselves—like this one—take months of strenuous effort to accomplish. But those who deplore the lightning-quick transmissions and reactions that have so sped up our lives and tightened deadlines might take some comfort from the reflection that at least we're not fighting battles anymore these days after the wars have ended.

On the other hand, some of us still are: twenty percent of all veterans returning from combat deployments, according to the Department of Defense. Which is what brought these hikers to the Appalachian Trail and consumed several months of their lives.

The story of the trail itself begins just after the First World War. The Industrial Revolution and urbanization had by then pretty much separated most Americans from what remained of their forests and wild lands. The Weeks Act of 1911, complementing the efforts of President Roosevelt to preserve the nation's natural treasures, as well as the creation of the Adirondack Forest Preserve and the White Mountain National Forest, had done much to preserve or reclaim precious wilderness lands. And the idea of a foot trail connecting Mount Mitchell in the Smoky Mountains with the geologically related peak of Mount Washington in the White Mountains was a gleam in the eye of a few avid "trampers," as they called them then.

In 1921, Benton MacKaye, a sometime editor, forester, and government employee, first articulated the idea in writing in an article titled "An Appalachian Trail: A Project in Regional Planning," which appeared in the *Journal of the American Institute of Architects.* Apparently, he wasn't so much a hiker as a visionary. He proposed it as a series of work camps scattered along the main Appalachian ridge, in which city-weary young people could get away from the factories and urban blight. The camps would be connected by the trail that they would build. Boring.

MacKaye's idea caught on, but hardly in the way he intended; he was trampled by a stampede of hiking boots as people signed on. First, his plan for the trail was extended from Georgia to Maine. A group of volunteers dug in and built a section near where the trail would cross the Hudson River in New York. In 1925 the first Appalachian Trail Conference was held. But the actual building languished for another three years, until the pressure to connect the finished sections brought the hikers out in force, and new, energetic leaders emerged. By 1937 the trail was laid out and mostly marked, though much of it was at the sufferance of private landowners. Nobody, as far as anybody knows, had yet conceived of hiking the entire trail; it was used mostly by day-hikers.

We're skipping a lot of history here in order to get to Earl Shaffer, a veteran of World War II in the Pacific, who in 1948 took to the trail in Georgia, telling friends he needed to "walk off the war." Four months later, he informed the incredulous leaders of the AT Conference that he had completed it. Eventually he proved it, and the tradition of "thru-hiking" had begun. Today thousands take to the trail each year, and hundreds manage to finish it.

Which brings us to the group that just celebrated their successful thru-hike in Millinocket. They're veterans of recent wars in Iraq, Afghanistan, and Somalia. The so-called "Warrior Hike" is the

brainchild of retired Marine Captain Sean Gobin, who hiked the trail
in 2012 and rounded up fourteen veterans to try it this year. The four
who made it last Friday are the trail-tough survivors of what must
have at times felt like a cavalry charge.

The New Hampshire Public Television crew and I met them the
morning of August 15 at the foot of Smarts Mountain, near Lyme
Center, New Hampshire, and climbed a little over halfway up the
mountain with them, talking and filming as we went. There were five
of them then—Tom, Steve, and Rob from the Army and Marines;
Stephanie, a "hull maintenance technician" from the Navy; and Sha-
ron "Mama Goose," an Air Force field medic.

I lived either on or very near the Appalachian Trail for forty years,
and have met hundreds of hikers. These were different: They were
peppier, better clothed, and they smelled a lot better than the average
thru-hiker. I figured out why when I saw on their Facebook page the
list of eager American Legion chapters that had hosted them along

the way. But they were adapted to the trail. When we stopped for lunch on a ledge with a view of the pyramid of the mountain, Stephanie whipped out a tiny stove and within a couple of minutes had boiled up a hot lunch of pasta and tomato sauce. They cooked separately, hiked together much of the time, and congregated for appointments like the one with us, or for potluck suppers along the way. "You have to hike your own hike," Tom pronounced, but they anticipated camping together that night, a few miles farther up the trail on the other side of the mountain looming above us. After a bit, they slipped on their hefty packs and headed up the the first of the significant White Mountain foothills. They were just beginning the hardest miles of the 2,000-mile trek; but they'd already had lots of hard miles behind them before they even started. There was no question they'd make it. And now they have.

A Hike to a Long-Ago Plane Crash

North Woodstock, New Hampshire
November 2013

Fewer and fewer people are now alive who remember the rank anxiety that gripped the United States at the beginning of 1942. Just before Christmas in 1941, planes and submarines of the Japanese navy had attacked Pearl Harbor. Four days later, Germany and its ally Italy, who judged (mistakenly, as it turned out) that Japan would make short work of the United States and would then help Germany defeat the Soviet Union, also declared war on us. Suddenly our two oceans didn't seem the barrier to attack they had been.

After the surprise at Pearl Harbor, no threat seemed unlikely. German submarines were active just off the coast of New England, sinking shipments of food and materiel to Great Britain and the Soviets. The Office of Civil Defense began installing wailing air raid warning sirens on tall buildings and appointing neighborhood air raid wardens; radio spots urged us to keep our mouths shut in public and report anything suspicious; "The Fifth Column," those among us whom

we imagined to be working to betray us, became a national obsession.

It was against this backdrop that an Army Air Force B-18A bomber took off from Westover Air Force Base in western Massachusetts on January 14 for an antisubmarine patrol down the Atlantic coast to the vicinity of Newfoundland and back. The B-18, a military version of the Douglas DC-2, was already on the verge of obsolescence in 1942, and was soon to be replaced by faster and better-armed bombers; but its slow cruising speed was an advantage in antisubmarine warfare. It carried, on this mission, 300-pound bombs. If it had an Achilles heel, it was probably its crew: A pickup group of men trained in the faster, larger, and better equipped B-24, they were not old crewmates. And, though it may be difficult to appreciate now, they were what we would call kids. The combination of the threat of war and the romance of flight had drawn thousands of young men, many just out of high school, into combat flight responsibilities.

A group of us gathered this morning at the beginning of the trail to the wreckage marking the end of that ill-fated mid-January flight. Besides the New Hampshire Public Television film crew of Steve and Phil, we had the family—father, mother, and two young boys—that had won this year's "A Day with the Crew" auction, and Sarah, a National Forest Service archeologist and site interpreter. The wreckage is on federal land, and there's no official trail to it, in an effort to preserve it from degradation—for some reason, a lot of people seem to want a piece of charred aluminum or an ancient spark plug as a memento—and part of her job was to remind us of that. The site is a memorial to the young airmen who died there long ago.

There was a bit of snow on the ground at the start of our climb, promising more farther up—the trail climbs an impressive 1,100 feet in just over half a mile—so I tucked my studded creepers into my pack, a very wise act, as it turned out.

As the bomber droned back toward Massachusetts on that dark January evening, it ran into heavy winds and snow squalls. The navigator had no way to measure the plane's drift and was now dictating the course by dead reckoning. It's hard for us to imagine now, with our advanced radar, global positioning devices, and satellite communications, how difficult it was then. The old maxim was, that if you didn't know where you were, it was impossible to know how to get to where you wanted to go. Through a break in the clouds, the crew spotted the lights of a city. Providence, Rhode Island, the navigator reckoned, and set a course for Westover. But the city they saw was Concord, New Hampshire, and they were now headed toward the White Mountains. When the wings began icing, the pilot dropped down to 3,800 feet, below the level of the unsuspected peaks.

Francianna Huot of North Woodstock stepped onto her porch and heard a roar overhead. Looking up, she briefly saw an American bomber—the old marking was a white star in a blue circle with a red "meatball" in the middle of the star—and a few minutes later heard the concussion of the crash. Everybody in town heard it, and then two more explosions. After several hurried phone calls, rescue teams began to assemble for the trek up the mountain toward the bright flames.

I tried to imagine, as I struggled up the steep path toward the wreck, what it was like for the first rescue party to do that in a snowstorm in the dark, with one flashlight and a kerosene lantern among them, through a couple of feet of snow, and hindered by the jackstrawed timber felled by the Hurricane of 1938. They shouted as they climbed, heard finally some faint cries for help, and met three injured men, in bloody flight suits and suffering from shock, straggling down the mountain toward the lights they'd spotted in the valley. Some rescuers guided them down toward the next parties, which had toboggans and first aid equipment, and the rest continued up to the blaze, where they found two more men alive. Two men were trapped and dead in the fiery wreckage.

Sarah's GPS gave us on demand the distance to the site. In my head, I looked at the slope and calculated instead the hypotenuse: The 500 yards on the GPS translated to about 700 yards of climbing. But at length we came to a large radial engine and spotted above us the flash of an American flag. The plane's copilot had at the last moment tried to raise its nose, and turned hard right, so that, instead of slamming head-first into the slope, it had plowed at a low angle into the birch forest, scattering parts everywhere, but preserving a few lives.

There are now a pair of memorial plaques there, and a dozen or so tiny American flags stuck into the soil. We ate our sandwiches in the snow, amid somber memories of a long-ago war.

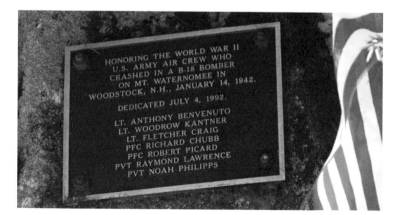

The Emerald Necklace
Boston, Massachusetts
July 2014

The New Hampshire Public Television crew and I stood this morning beside a couple of fortresslike granite buildings with nineteenth-century-style hip roofs, ocher-colored grout, and fancy exposed rafter tails. They were designed, a brochure informs me, by the famous architect Henry Hobson Richardson. There was water on one side of the buildings: an imperceptibly flowing stream named, appropriately, the Muddy River. Both banks of the stream were lush with greenery; Canada geese paddled about leisurely, tipping their bottoms comically into the air as they fed. On the other side, a few yards away, Boston drivers channeled their favorite Formula I drivers as they raced by on the Fenway.

We were in a park named Back Bay Fens, a part of the so-called Emerald Necklace that swings in a big arc around South Boston. Just a few blocks away, but obscured from us by foliage and tall apartment hous-

es, rises Fenway Park. The Emerald Necklace is a string of nine loosely connected parks, most of them designed by the famous landscape architect Frederick Law Olmsted, whose signature accomplishment was Central Park in New York City.

I've long been suspicious of guys who use all three of their names—Frank Lloyd Wright, Andrew Lloyd Webber, John Wilkes Booth, and James Earl Ray, for example—but have to admit that Richardson and Olmsted created a wonder here, a veritable silk purse from a sow's ear. The Muddy River, before Olmsted persuaded the City of Boston to take it in hand, was essentially an open sewer. Noisome and pestilential as it was, it was also largely ignored because it was flushed twice daily by the tide in the Charles River Estuary.

Hired by Boston shortly after the Civil War to design parks preserving green space, Olmsted insisted on incorporating the reclamation of the Muddy in the design. The river was dammed near here in the fens, shutting out the salt water and providing a modicum of flood control: One of the granite buildings is still a gatehouse regulating the flow of

Stony Brook, a tributary now running through an aqueduct beneath the streets of Boston. Then he created a series of ponds, including some existing glacial kettleholes, and enhanced their connection to the Muddy.

We visited four of the parks in the necklace today. At each one we were greeted by volunteer docents or other lovers of the greenbelt. It was hard not to be impressed by their enthusiasm for the place. All of them expressed their delight with such a peaceful place, where it was possible to get away from the stress of the urban hustle and bustle all around. I felt a slight disconnect there. I live in a state that's pretty much a park already—that's getting back its forests naturally as agriculture declines and large-scale logging gets smarter—and couldn't help hearing the roar of the city always in the background. In recording studios, technicians have to turn off the air conditioning, no matter how quiet, or it's audible in the result. These parks, peaceful as they are, feature of necessity a constant reminder of what you're escaping.

As we strolled from the gatehouse to a picturesque bridge over the Muddy, a pair of walkers appeared who for some reason had numbers on their chests. Then three more; then dozens; and finally a parade of hundreds. Some walked with canes, one with crutches, and another was in a wheelchair. It was apparently a benefit walk supporting Home Base, a Red Sox initiative to aid returning servicemen. Around the edges of the column of walkers, bicyclists zipped here and there, among dozens of joggers and strolling couples. Not many couples, however, were lounging lazily on the lawns, even on a Saturday; the geese had gotten there first.

At the end of our trip through the Back Bay Fens, we bade adieu to our cheerful docents (the docents in the parks tend to be knowledgeable academics; one of this pair was a wetlands scientist and the other a landscape architect), and moved on to Olmsted Park, where a seventy-nine-year-old naturalist and active hiker showed us a pond

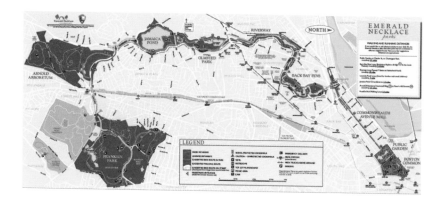

about to be dredged to increase its volume for flood control, a brook named Babbling—though in this dry summer it's better called Murmuring—and another, natural kettlehole pond formed when a buried mass of ice melted a few thousand years ago. Two younger docents, one a botanist, showed us specimens of invasive species they'd tagged to be uprooted by volunteer "Green Team" youth workers.

Then it was on to the Arnold Arboretum, managed by Harvard and the City of Boston, and home to about 15,000 species of trees and shrubs. There are Asian and American tamaracks here bigger than any I've ever seen before, a couple of dawn redwoods, and an Asian species of sequoia (if I have it right) that had long been considered extinct until two of them were discovered by chance in China a few years ago. The specimens here were started from seeds sent from China. The whole arboretum has the feel of a living museum.

Our last stop was Franklin Park, the largest gem in the necklace. It's the liveliest, too, with an eighteen-hole golf course, a zoo, and large picnic areas with—as we discovered—electrical hookups for amplifiers and microphones for large parties. My guide here was Dan Richardson, a seventy-five-year-old man and Hero Volunteer Award winner who's lived his life beside the park. As we hobbled with our canes across a road to get to Schoolmaster Hill, we laughed about the fantastic scene in *Bowfinger,* where director Steve Martin sends Eddie Murphy across the Los Angeles Freeway in rush-hour traffic. But we made it all right, too, and soon were sitting on a stone wall above the golf course. As we chatted, a broad-winged hawk climbed out of the trees behind Dan, grabbed a small songbird out of the air, and headed back to its nest and kids with afternoon tea. A perfect symbol for the Emerald Necklace: wild creatures living free in the midst of a huge, churning city.

Interesting People
Montpelier, Vermont
September 2014

One of the nicest things about my current part-time job is that it gets me outdoors, as well as all over the map, to particular places I'd probably otherwise never have visited: mountains, rivers, and lakes, and what New Hampshire calls the Great North Woods, or on some of its signs, *les Bois du Grand Nord*.

But the greatest pleasure for me is the people I get to meet. They're mountaineers, canoeists, hikers, bird-watchers, naturalists, and program directors engaged in what Calvin Coolidge once called "service to others." They cheerfully put up with my doddering glacial pace on the trail, and sit still for my Ancient Mariner style of storytelling. They're happy, upbeat, and excited about what they're doing. What's not to like about all that?

The weather gods do not always smile upon our scheduled ap-

pointments. But I've heretofore consoled myself that conditions can't possibly be too tough: that whatever the big video camera can withstand, I can, too. But lately the New Hampshire Public Television team is using, in difficult conditions, the new GoPro camera, a tiny (and waterproof) digital device that shoots amazingly good images. So I'm having to rethink my own limits. My mantra has had to change from "What the camera can stand, I can," to "Well, I haven't dissolved yet, and probably won't."

You will no doubt remember the fierce wind-and-rain storm that blew through Vermont and New Hampshire in the middle of the second week of August this year. The crew and I had planned to spend a couple of days with a group of young people engaged in a program called On Belay. The forecast for the first day looked fine—warm and sunny—but a huge, swirling storm would move in late that evening with gale-force winds and drenching rain. We checked with the folks at On Belay; they'd be there, they said. So we went, too.

We stayed overnight at the Appalachian Mountain Club's newish Highland Center Lodge, just north of Crawford Notch, where winds funneling through the Notch burst out into the open. That first day, in warm sunshine, we and the kids hiked Mount Willard, an easy mountain with a great view, and scampered back down to the Notch well before supper. They had more meetings afterward—it's quite a job to whip a mixed bunch of high school-age kids into a safe, cooperative group—and we all went to bed just as the tempest broke over the valley.

On Belay was founded in 2004 by a New Hampshire mother of two girls who was diagnosed with breast cancer. Concerned that during her aggressive therapy the girls' needs would be shunted onto a side track, she put together the beginnings of an outdoor adventure program for her kids and others from families similarly afflicted. The name is the phrase that roped-together climbers use when one's about to climb, and the other is secure and ready to help or catch a fall. The program isn't therapy in the traditional sense; it's simply a chance for kids with the same stressful experiences to share them, even if only tacitly, and have fun together outdoors. It's free of charge, thanks to generous donors, and the AMC provides the necessary equipment gratis, as well.

It was still pouring and blowing hard at breakfast time, but the gang packed up and with their leaders headed up the soggy Crawford Path toward Mizpah Hut. We left them about halfway up, sloshed back down to our vehicles, and headed north to the second of our week's adventures.

We spent the night in Happy Corner, New Hampshire, where we've been before. I like it for its home-style café and the general store, where the guys getting early-morning coffee are very friendly. But we were there to meet Buffalo and Tough Cookie.

This duo with the colorful nicknames are Dan Szczesny (pronouncing his name is like standing an egg on end: easy if you know how) and Janelle. He's the associate publisher of *The Hippo*, a large weekly newspaper that serves southern New Hampshire; she's his thirteen-year-old climbing partner.

About five years ago a pair of twins, Aaron and Janelle, moved in with their grandparents next door to Dan and his wife's house. They visited often; and when the grandfather died and Dan's wife lost her job, the kids sort of adopted the Szczesnys. What could they do, Dan wondered, to keep these kids occupied? Dan's default mode is hiking: He's done the White Mountain 4,000-footers and trekked to Base

Camp on Everest. So he took them hiking.

Aaron's response was friendly, but tepid. Janelle's, however, was over the moon. She wanted to go again. Dan allowed they could if they could coordinate with the others from that first hike. "That's OK," she said. "You can just take me."

And so he did. They've hiked the so-called "Fifty-Two with a View," and Dan's written a book about it, using their trail names: *The Adventures of Buffalo and Tough Cookie*. Together, we skipped up (well, she did; I plodded) Mount Magalloway, just short of the Canadian border. On the summit we shared a thermos of tea that Dan always carries. Janelle was barely warmed up. Having danced lightly up the mountainside, she ran back down.

Dan and Janelle both claimed to have enjoyed the experience a lot. I don't know how they could have enjoyed it more than I. The mountains have started something in that young lady. I hope I'm around to see where it leads. Yep, I meet really interesting people.

Mountain Day at Colby-Sawyer College

New London, New Hampshire
October 2014

It happens once a year, and with only a couple of minor breaks, has been happening for over 150 years. It's Mountain Day at Colby-Sawyer College. Its date is always a well-kept secret among a few administrators and professors, but our crew had been let in on it so we could be here to climb the mountain with the students and film the event.

I have no idea how many schools have mountain days. My northern Massachusetts school had one, and still does: a day whose date is secret, and upon which the senior class is excused from everything else, bussed to the foot of Mount Monadnock, and treated after their descent to burgers and hotdogs at the campground, with the faculty doing the honors in chef's hats. It's the same deal here at Colby-Sawyer, but here it's Mount Kearsarge, and the whole school climbs.

Colby-Sawyer has gone through many changes in its long life, be-

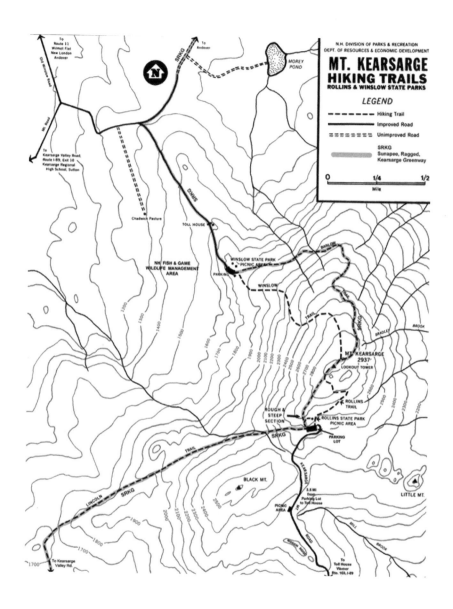

ginning as an academy founded and funded by the Colbys, a prominent local family. It was for many years during the mid-twentieth
century a women's institution known as Colby Junior College. Many
Dartmouth alums of my vintage recall it as a happy hunting ground;

they practically wore grooves in the secondary roads between Hanover and New London—the interstate highway system was still only a gleam in Dwight Eisenhower's eye—and not a few of them found wives here. Dartmouth, however, became coeducational in 1972 and Colby in 1991; thus, in spite of the increased ease of travel, the volume has no doubt diminished.

The thought of hundreds of young people with still incomplete cortical restraints clambering over miles of steep, rough trails must give administrators heart palpitations. Last year at Colby-Sawyer, four students came back down with injuries needing treatment. But the college encourages the climb every year—at the same time choosing the best possible weather and footing for the event.

Why do they do it? Simply because extracurricular activity is the best way to build institutional solidarity. The friends you make on the touch football field will outlast every time those sitting next to you in English class. The ones you hike, climb, canoe, or mountain bike with last even longer. My old buddy, the late Dudley Weider, often said that the fellow alums he remained closest to were the men he'd met on his Freshman Trip.

Still an institution at Dartmouth, First-Year Trips (they dropped "freshman" because of its sexist overtone possibilities) engages about ninety percent of entering students. They clamber, bike, ride horses, and paddle all over northern New Hampshire, camping along the way, and finish with a raucous dinner at the college's Moosilauke Ravine Lodge near the foot of the mountain. The college's rugged identity is firmly implanted there. I used to go to those dinners whenever I could, just to watch the speakers, college officials accustomed to dry presentations, trying to catch hold of the students' enthusiasm, like late-arriving travelers boarding an accelerating train.

A couple of female students, interviewed for an article in the college daily, explained it well: "I wanted to take advantage of the great

location Hanover was in and try new outdoor activities like whitewater kayaking that I never tried before college," said one. The other: "I
knew I wanted to go to a school where I could be outside all the time,
because that's how I recharge psychologically, academically, emotion-
ally," she said.

Colby-Sawyer is in an equally rich environment. Mount Kearsarge,
a 2,920-foot granite monadnock with a summit left bald by a 1796 forest fire, looms over the campus. The annual climb is the ideal way to
get students together—on the buses, on the trail, at the top, at the barbecue after the descent. It's also a way, I discerned during the climb, to
introduce foreign students to this beautiful part of the United States.
On the summit, I chatted with three young women sharing a cigarette,
one from Macedonia and two from Nepal, and had my picture taken
with another from Nigeria who was climbing with a new friend from
Massachusetts. Others were up in the fire tower, checking out the story
that on a clear day they might see the towers of Boston. Faculty and

staff members were practically indistinguishable from the students, which on a day like today is a good thing.

We had fun before the climb talking about the ways the students try to predict the exact day of the event. They go at it with the sophistication of a bookmaker or hedge fund administrator. Some check the president's published schedule; if he's away, it won't happen, because he always climbs. They check the weather forecasts; it won't be on a rainy day, and probably not the day after. Someone came up with the bright idea that the kitchen staff, preparing for the afternoon barbecue al fresco, take the ketchup bottles off the dining hall tables early that morning. But once that idea became known, it was rumored the kitchen staff began taking away the bottles randomly, just to confuse the issue. Students who know which professors are in on the secret watch them covertly for changes in behavior or dress. Hiking shoes, in some cases, are a giveaway.

However it is, shortly after ten o'clock in the morning the traditional designated bell-ringer makes his way to the college bell tower and peals out the news. This being 2014, there's another means of instant communication: the all-college text message. Within minutes this morning, students began congregating under the maples at the edge of the quad where the buses would pick them up. Shortly after that, we joined a fast-moving mob streaming up the short, rocky 1.1-mile trail to the top. Watching them practically leap uphill, I wished myself able to trade some of my hard-won prudence for just a little of that long-lost mountain goat agility. It's been a lovely day.

This Mountain Stands Alone in Memory Too

Jaffrey, New Hampshire
October 2014

On a Thursday morning in October, the first intimation that the hike ahead of us might not be a solitary one was the full parking lot at the foot of the mountain. Mount Monadnock is apparently one of the world's most-climbed mountains. Weekend traffic here must be fierce.

Turns out it is. Larry, our genial, garrulous guide, told us that when the mountain is busiest, the rangers institute one-way traffic on the two most popular trails—one for uphill, the other for down. Still, there are frequent traffic jams at two or three rock pitches that require scrambling on all fours, sometimes after a bit of deliberation.

As our party of eight started up the lower section of the main trail, it felt familiar to me, and I remembered I'd been here twice before, in

October of 1952 and 1985. I also remembered that in 1952 I wanted to be the first of my high school class to make it to the top, and ran up the mountain. Today, I was just hoping to get there—and get back down in one piece.

It's only 2.2 miles from the trailhead to the 3,165-foot-high summit, but there's an 1,800-foot climb, most of it in the second mile. A little before the halfway mark, a clear, cold spring bubbled out of the mountainside through a steel pipe. Just after that, even though I was ready for it, the trail tilted upward like a barn roof, and then out of sight in the trees, in a most breathtaking way. Time to shorten my hiking poles and shift into trudge mode.

Translations of Native American languages into any others is always tricky and often imprecise; but the consensus about the meaning of the Abenaki word, "monadnock," is that it means "mountain that stands alone." Which it certainly does: There's not another anywhere near it. The term has become the geological generic for any similar isolated mountain. Considering that New Hampshire was at least once submerged under continental ice sheets that scoured, plucked, and deposited rock, sand, and gravel everywhere, it's easy to conclude that the bulk of Mount Monadnock was harder and more resistant than the surrounding bedrock.

Sure enough, the first thing I noticed—after the sudden steepening of the slope—was the hardness of the rock. It's heavily metamorphosed schist and quartzite of the so-called Littleton Formation, which achieved its present composition during the great clash of the North American and Eurasian tectonic plates about 400 million years ago. What happened here is best illustrated by pushing a scatter rug from both ends; it forms up-folds and down-folds. There are many of those here on Monadnock. The largest is a downfold (syncline) that's tipped over on its side. Geology students can have a field day doping out the mountain's history—or losing their minds trying to.

My carbide steel-tipped hiking poles that bite so beautifully in White Mountain granite, slid sideways now and then and left me teetering for balance. Mount Cube in Orford is similar: shiny with glacial polish and laced with veins of milky quartz. Naturally, the rubber tips that fit onto my poles, and would have been a big help, were home in a drawer. On the bright side, however, the composition of the soles of modern hiking shoes is almost like glue in its stickiness; where the slabs were dry, the traction was great.

The New Hampshire Public Television crew and I were here to film a story about Larry Davis, a fiftyish, ponytailed athlete who claims over 6,000 ascents of Monadnock, including a stretch of 2,850 consecutive days (almost eight years) until pneumonia stopped the streak. He still climbs it nearly daily, bicycling half an hour to the base from his apartment in Jaffrey. He and his friends—two of them here with us today—carry plastic bags and collect every bit of trash they spot on the mountain. The combination of their efforts and a growing environmental awareness among hikers has led to a major reduction.

The mountain has taken its lumps over the millennia. After its tortured nativity, it existed as a moderate eminence until the ice sheets arrived and bulldozed almost everything in their path. Its "upstream" slope is scoured clean and grooved with striations; its downstream side is piled high with boulders and fragments dumped as the ice went by. Native Americans had little interest in mountaineering; besides, spirits often inhabited the summits. The first recorded ascent was made in 1725 by a Captain Samuel Willard and fourteen British-American rangers on an Indian-hunting trip. They used the summit as a lookout—for the smoke of campfires, I presume.

There was lots of smoke here about seventy-five years later, when Yankee sheep farmers set the red spruce forest ablaze to clear the land for pasture. Later, convinced that the remaining forest concealed predators, they burned that, too, between 1810 and 1820; the mountain's top 1,000 feet has been bald ever since. Nowadays, more than 125,000 hikers annually stream up and down the trails, with amazingly little wear and tear—the result, probably, of volunteer maintenance (Larry, for example, showed me a stretch of trail in boggy ground near the summit, that he had paved with large flat rocks) and the prevalence of bedrock ledges, which are hard to wear out.

We climbed through mountain ash and mountain cranberry and reached the cold, windy summit in early afternoon. The demands of the cameras, both television and still, and the severity of the perilous descent—I think I prayed and gasped a lot—slowed us down considerably; we reached the parking lot just as the last light faded from the sky and the trail beneath our feet became indistinct. I think we were the last people down. The mountain loomed above us under a bright rising moon. I took a long, long look. Unlike Larry Davis, I may never get up there again.

Permissions

Photographs

All photographs courtesy of New Hampshire Public Television, except:

Front cover, p. 12: Jerry Monkman, EcoPhotography

pages 2, 10: Lisa Nugent

page 16: Chris Sanfino

page 22: Michael Tsai, http://hiking.mjtsai.com

pages 41, 43: Courtesy of the Lange family

pages 73, 75: Schuyler Scribner

page 80: Courtesy of Don Vandenburgh

page 129: Erik Gehring

page 130: Courtesy of The Emerald Necklace Conservancy

pages 134, 135, 152: Joe Klementovich Photography

pages 139, 142, 143: Gil Talbot

pages 145, 146, 149: Adam Goodine Photography

page 156: Brent Doscher Photography

Maps

page 19: Courtesy of Upper Valley Lake Sunapee Regional Planning Commission

pages 21: Detail of *White Mountain Trail Map 2: Franconia–Pemigewasset,*
      © 2012 Appalachian Mountain Club

page 27: Detail of *White Mountain Trail Map 3: Carter Range–Evans Notch*
      Appalachian Mountain Club

page 33: Detail of *Maine Mountain Trail Map 2: 100-Mile Wilderness*
      © 2012 Appalachian Mountain Club

page 64: Detail of *White Mountain Trail Map 1: Presidential Range*
      © 2012 Appalachian Mountain Club

page: 106: from *AMC's Best Day Hikes in Vermont* by Jennifer Lamphere Roberts,
      Map by Ken Dumas © 2013 Appalachian Mountain Club

pages 42, 59, 94: US Geological Survey maps

page 132: Courtesy of The Emerald Necklace Conservancy

page 140: New Hampshire Division of Parks & Recreation,
      Department of Resources and Economic Development

All photographs and maps not in the public domain used with permission.

Related *Windows to the Wild* Episodes

Acknowledgments

None of these stories or programs would have been possible without the help and support of a legion of companions. All of them have special places in my memories and in my heart.

A few in particular stand out:

The current crew of Steve Giordani, Phil Vaughn, Schuyler Scribner, and various hardy interns;

The original *Windows to the Wild* production crew of Marc Diessner, Jonathon Millman, Schuyler Scribner, Steve Giordani, Phil Vaughn, and Chip Neal;

All the people who have shared their knowledge, stories, and experiences on *Windows to the Wild* over the years;

The folks at New Hampshire Public Television who keep the program on the air in different ways: Peter Frid, Dawn DeAngelis, Hazel Molin, Montana West, Carla Gordon Russell, Schuyler Scribner, Susan Adams, Sarah Varney, and Bryn Burns;

Grace Lessner, who's been on the editorial trail of this book and promoting the program since its inception;

Rob Burbank and his colleagues at the Appalachian Mountain Club, who have led us on so many of the adventures we've shared on the program;

The team at Bauhan Publishing in Peterborough: Sarah Bauhan, Mary Ann Faughnan, Henry James, and Jocelyn Lovering, and Mike Ribaudo at Kase Printing who brought this book to fruition;

My wife, Ida, who has been on all kinds of trails with me for over fifty years;

The generous program sponsors and underwriters who've funded our adventures;

And, always, our viewers and fans, who keep us going.

Thank you.